FREE Test Taking Tips Video/DVD Offer

To better serve you, we created videos covering test taking tips that we want to give you for FREE. **These videos cover world-class tips that will help you succeed on your test.**

We just ask that you send us feedback about this product. Please let us know what you thought about it—whether good, bad, or indifferent.

To get your **FREE videos**, you can use the QR code below or email freevideos@studyguideteam.com with "Free Videos" in the subject line and the following information in the body of the email:

   a. The title of your product

   b. Your product rating on a scale of 1-5, with 5 being the highest

   c. Your feedback about the product

If you have any questions or concerns, please don't hesitate to contact us at info@studyguideteam.com.

Thank you!

CogAT Grade 2 Workbook

CogAT Form 8 with Practice Test
Questions for the Level 8 Exam
[Includes Detailed Answer Explanations]

Joshua Rueda

Interested in buying more than 10 copies of our product? Contact us about bulk discounts:
bulkorders@studyguideteam.com

ISBN 13: 9781637758489
ISBN 10: 1637758481

Table of Contents

Quick Overview *1*

Test-Taking Strategies *2*

FREE Videos/DVD OFFER *4*

Introduction *5*

Verbal *6*

Quantitative *9*

Nonverbal *13*

Practice Test *18*

Verbal 18

Quantitative 34

Nonverbal 47

Answer Explanations *107*

Verbal 107

Quantitative 110

Nonverbal 112

Quick Overview

As you draw closer to taking your exam, being prepared becomes more and more important. Thankfully, you have this study guide to help you get ready. Use this guide to help keep your preparation on track and refer to it often.

This study guide contains several key sections that will help you be successful on your exam. The guide has tips for what you should do the night before and the day of the test. Also included are test-taking tips. These tips will help equip you to read, assess, and answer test questions.

A large part of this guide is devoted to showing you what content to expect on the exam and to helping you better understand that content. We also show you practice test questions so that you can see how well you understand the content and how you might perform on the test. Then, answers are provided so that you can understand why you missed certain questions.

Be sure to go to bed at a reasonable time the night before your exam. Being well-rested helps you focus and remain calm. Be sure to eat a substantial breakfast the morning of the exam. If you are taking the exam in the afternoon, have a good lunch as well. Being hungry is distracting and can make it difficult to focus. You have hopefully spent lots of time preparing for the exam. Don't let an empty stomach get in the way of success!

Be sure to pace yourself during the exam. Don't try to rush. Allow yourself use of all the allotted time if needed.

Remain positive while taking the exam even if you feel like you are performing poorly. Thinking about the content you should have mastered will not help you perform better on the exam once it's started.

Once the exam is complete, take some time to relax. Even if you feel that you might need to take the exam again, you will be well served by some down time before you begin further preparation.

Test-Taking Strategies

1. Predicting the Answer

When you feel confident in your preparation for a multiple-choice test, try predicting the answer before looking at the answer choices. By predicting the answer before looking at the choices, you will less likely be distracted by an incorrect answer choice. You will feel more confident in your selection if you look at the question, predict the answer, and then find your prediction among the answer choices. After using this strategy, be sure to still look at the answer choices carefully and completely. If you feel unprepared, you should not attempt to predict the answers. This would be a waste of time and an opportunity for your mind to wander in the wrong direction.

2. Looking for Wrong Answers

One way to simplify multiple-choice question is to eliminate all answer choices that are clearly wrong. There will usually be at least one choice that can be dismissed right away. If the test is administered on paper, the test taker could draw a line through the incorrect answer to indicate that it may be ignored; otherwise, the test taker will have to perform this operation mentally or on scratch paper. In either case, once the obviously incorrect answers have been eliminated, the remaining choices may be considered.

3. Don't Overanalyze

When you are nervous, your brain will often run wild, causing you to make associations and discover clues that don't exist. If you feel that this may be a problem for you, do whatever you can to slow down during the test. Try taking a deep breath or counting to ten. Don't overthink the question.

4. No Need for Panic

It is wise to learn as many strategies as possible before taking a multiple-choice test, but it is likely that you will come across a few questions for which you don't know the answer. In this situation, avoid panicking. Getting one incorrect answer does not mean failure. When you find a question that you either don't understand or don't know how to answer, just take a deep breath and do your best. Consider the question and each answer choice slowly and carefully. After eliminating obviously wrong answers, make a selection and move on to the next question.

5. Your First Instinct

Many people struggle with multiple-choice tests because they overthink the questions. If you have studied for the test, be prepared to trust your first instinct once you have looked at the question and answer choices. There is a great deal of research suggesting that the mind can come to the correct conclusion quickly once it has obtained all of the relevant information. At times, it may seem as if your intuition is working faster even than your reasoning mind. This may in fact be true. The skills you obtain in preparation may be retrieved from your subconscious before you have a chance to work out the associations that support it. Verify your instinct by working out the reasons that it should be trusted.

6. Consider Every Answer Choice

It may seem obvious, but you should always look at every one of the answer choices! Too many test takers fall into the habit of answering too quickly. One answer choice may appear to be correct at first

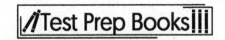

glance when in reality it's simply similar to the correct answer. Failing to consider all of the answer choices is like not reading all of the items on a restaurant menu: you might miss out on the perfect choice.

7. No Patterns

Answer choices will never be chosen based on patterns. The questions are scrambled and delivered in a random order. Any attempt to discern a pattern in the answer choices is a waste of time and a distraction from the real work of taking the test. A test taker would be much better served by extra preparation before the test than by reliance on a pattern in the answers.

FREE Videos/DVD OFFER

Doing well on your exam requires both knowing the test content and understanding how to use that knowledge to do well on the test. We offer completely FREE test taking tip videos. **These videos cover world-class tips that you can use to succeed on your test.**

To get your **FREE videos**, you can use the QR code below or email freevideos@studyguideteam.com with "Free Videos" in the subject line and the following information in the body of the email:

    a. The title of your product

    b. Your product rating on a scale of 1-5, with 5 being the highest

    c. Your feedback about the product

If you have any questions or concerns, please don't hesitate to contact us at info@studyguideteam.com.

Thanks again!

Introduction

Function and Administration

The Cognitive Abilities Test (CogAT) is a test used for entrance or placement decisions into gifted and talented programs and classes across the United States. The exam offers K–12 assessment in the areas of reasoning and problem-solving abilities through Verbal, Nonverbal, and Quantitative batteries.

Administration of the CogAT depends on the school district offering the test. Reach out to your school district to see when they offer the test and how to register for it. Retesting is also dependent on the school offering the exam. Many school districts do not offer the CogAT again in a single academic year once the student has taken the exam, but this may vary in different areas.

Test Format

The CogAT exam Grade 2 Level 8 is made up of 3 batteries: Verbal, Nonverbal, and Quantitative. Level 8 is for second grade students who are at the age of eight years old. The Level 8 CogAT has 154 questions. Administration of the test will vary with the school district. For example, some sections on the exam may be administered separately, or they might be administered all at once. Within the three batteries of Verbal, Nonverbal, and Quantitative are the following subsections:

- Verbal
    - Verbal Classification
    - Verbal Analogies
    - Sentence Completion
- Quantitative
    - Number Series
    - Number Puzzles
    - Number Analogies
- Nonverbal
    - Figure Matrices
    - Paper Folding
    - Figure Classification

Scoring

Students do not lose points for guessing incorrectly, so students should always mark an answer on the CogAT exam even if they are not sure it's correct. There are several different ways to look at scores in the CogAT exam. The raw score shows the number of answers guessed correctly out of the number of questions. The Universal Scale Score (USS) is the three scores for the batteries, and then that is converted into one Composite score. The Standard Age Score (SAS) has a maximum score of 160 and shows the potential and rate of development of that student. The Percentile Rank (PR) is used to compare the student to others in their age and grade. Finally, the Stanine (S) score is simplified on a scale from 1 to 9 and normalized for ages and grades.

Recent/Future Developments

The latest version of the CogAT is the CogAT Form 8, which was developed with non-native English speakers in mind. CogAT Form 8 is considered equivalent to the CogAT Form 7.

Verbal

Picture/Verbal Classification

Description

In the Verbal Classification section of the Grade 2 CogAT test, the student's ability to read and recognize similarities will be tested. These questions give three words that are in some way alike or related. Students must recognize the similarity and apply it to choose one word from the multiple choice options at the end of the problem. Some questions may list a set of words that name three colors. In this problem, students must choose the answer that is also a color. These questions differ from the previous levels because students are given words instead of pictures at this stage.

Relevance

The relevance of this section can be seen in how students are learning to read and recognize ideas that are related. Students are required to not only read the words but comprehend what they mean and relate them to the others. This applies in life when students have choices to make. When told about the weather, they should be able to evaluate what types of clothes to wear that go along with being comfortable outside. If the weather is cold, they should associate that idea with a jacket and gloves. If the weather is warm, they should recognize that they will not need a hat and gloves to go outside but may need to wear lighter clothes to be comfortable.

Tips for Parents

One way to prepare students for this section is to write down some ideas, make a list of words that relate to that idea, and then present them to the student. One idea might be shapes. The list of words could be *circle*, *triangle*, and *square*. The parent could give this list to the student and ask for a fourth word that would relate in the same way that these are related. Some answers may be *rectangle*, *oval*, or *pentagon*.

It may also be helpful to discuss with the student what they see as the relation between the words. After identifying the relation, the student may come up with even more words that would also fit into the group. To provide a deeper understanding, the parent could ask the student to come up with a set of words and present them to the parent. Once the parent gives an answer, they can discuss the relation that they each see in the words. Any type of arguing or discussion to prove an answer correct is helpful in obtaining a deeper knowledge of the subject.

Sample Problem

The following problem is a sample of what students might see in the Verbal Classification section of the test.

        car   van   jeep

   A.   truck   B. door   C. window   D. lights

Explanation of Sample Problem

This sample problem gives a list of words that are related. These words are all types of vehicles. Once the relation is recognized, the answer can be chosen as another type of vehicle. The correct answer is A, truck. The other answers are all parts on a vehicle. While they relate to vehicles, they do not name types of vehicles, so they do not qualify as answers.

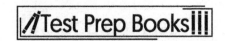

Picture/Verbal Analogies

Description

In the Verbal Analogies section of the Grade 2 CogAT test, the student's ability to recognize relationships and apply them is tested. The student will be given three words. The first two words will be related. The third word will be related to one of the answer choices. Once the student determines how the first two words are related, they can apply this same relationship to the third word in order to make an answer choice.

This section is more about individual relationships than groups of words, as in Verbal Classification. Students may be given the words *hungry*, *food*, and *thirsty*. The first two are related because providing food to someone makes them no longer hungry. Applying this concept to thirsty, the next word may be *drink* because this would make someone no longer thirsty.

Relevance

These types of relational ideas may prove useful to students as they make decisions. They may see their parents make healthy food choices and then recognize the health benefits that they have because of it. In turn, they may choose to make healthy food choices so that they will see the benefits also.

This can also be helpful in recognizing bad behavior and the consequences. If a student sees another student talk out of turn and lose a privilege, they may make a choice to not talk out of turn so that they also do not lose a privilege. This type of reasoning is very helpful in the growth and development of children.

Tips for Parents

One tip for this section is to emphasize to students what the questions are asking. Make sure that students know that the first two words are related, and that the third word is related to an answer. The format of the question should lend itself to this understanding, but there are so many different types of questions presented.

As with the other sections, practicing these types of questions is also helpful. Parents may give students an example of three words and then allow students to choose the fourth word. They may also talk through the relationships and have students make up two more words that are related in the same way.

Sample Problem

The following problem is a sample of what students might see in the Verbal Classification section of the test.

      Open: Close   Up:

  A. Over   B. Down   C. Left   D. Top

Explanation of Sample Problem

The relationship between the first two words is that they are opposites of each other. The opposite of opening a door is closing it. The third word is *up*, which is the opposite of *down*, Choice B. The other choices may be related to the third word, but they are not opposites.

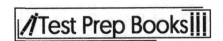

Sentence Completion

<u>Description</u>
In the Sentence Completion section of the Grade 2 CogAT test, the student's ability to comprehend ideas and complete open-ended questions is tested. Each question in this section consists of a sentence that is missing a word. The student must read and comprehend the sentence before choosing the best word to complete the sentence.

The main point of this section is for students to read and comprehend the topic of each sentence. Once they identify what is happening in the sentence, they can choose what word is best to complete each thought. The answer choices will be multiple choice, so students must be able to identify which words make sense in the sentence and which ones do not.

<u>Relevance</u>
Sentence completion may be the most complex of the verbal sections. It encompasses the ideas of understanding vocabulary, understanding relationships between words, and comprehension of more complex ideas. As students read the sentence, they are required to define the words in their head. They will then determine relationships between these words. The relationships can be generalized to form a final idea that explains the entire sentence. Each part of this process teaches students the importance of words and how they are used even in everyday conversation.

<u>Tips for Parents</u>
One of the best ways to help prepare for this type of problem is for students to read. Reading allows them to develop their comprehension skills and help them to become familiar with more complex words. While reading, students must understand sentences in context, and they must also apply their knowledge of vocabulary terms. The more they read, the more they develop their overall verbal skills.

Parents may also choose to write sentences with missing words in them. They can work with students to review meanings of words and discuss concepts within each sentence. As with the other verbal sections, it may also be helpful to discuss why some words would and would not fit into a sentence. All of these strategies will help students prepare for the Sentence Completion portion of the test.

<u>Sample Problem</u>
      The family was _____ from their long trip and decided to go straight to bed.

  A. hungry   B. energized   C. tired   D. thirsty

<u>Explanation of Sample Problem</u>
The sentence is talking about a family who has just been on a long trip. The end of the sentence explains that they go straight to bed. Since the result is the family going to bed, the choice of word must relate to this idea. The answer is C, tired. The family is tired, which results in them going straight to bed.

Quantitative

Number Series

Description
In the Number Series section of the Grade 2 CogAT test, the student's problem-solving ability will be tested as they reason through a given series of numbers. These numbers will be given in a specific order, and the students will determine the pattern used to find each successive number. Students will then apply this pattern or operation to the last number to find the next number in the series.

Some examples of operations may be adding five, or subtracting three, each time. Patterns may also include doubling the given number, or taking half of it, to find the next number in the sequence. There may also be more complex patterns that include adding twice the previous number to find the next number. Each question will have different patterns or operations, but the goal of finding the next number in the series is the same throughout this section.

Relevance
This section is relevant to students because it requires critical thinking skills. They must use their prior knowledge to recognize how the numbers relate to one another. This type of skill is important across all aspects of life as students work to be better problem-solvers. They will use their prior knowledge of sports and build upon it with new knowledge to become better athletes. They will use critical thinking skills to work out problems in their personal life when they have issues with friends instead of just giving up on a friendship. These skills will prove helpful in many aspects of life.

Tips for Parents
It is important that students recognize the objective of each section of the test. For this section, students will be expected to choose the next number in a series of numbers. Parents may start by introducing their child to a given series and asking them what pattern they recognize. If the student struggles at first, parents can offer help in finding the first pattern. They can then explain how to use an operation to find the next number.

It is also important to encourage practice. As students are exposed to more and more series, they will expand their knowledge and develop their problem-solving ability. Parents should come alongside students as they work through these questions, as they may not be accustomed to this type of problem.

Sample Problem
The following problem is a sample of what students might see in the Number Series section of the test.

| 2 | 4 | 8 | 16 | __ |

A. 20   B. 24   C. 32   D. 64

Explanation of Sample Problem
The answer to the sample problem is C. Since the problem given is a series of numbers, the student should recognize that the answer is the next number in the series. Students should recognize that the numbers increase each time, but not by the same amount. To get from one number to the next, the given number is doubled. The pattern for this series is x2, x2, x2, ... Using this same pattern and applying it to the last number, sixteen is doubled to yield thirty-two. The answer is C because sixteen multiplied

9

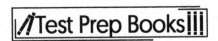

by two is thirty-two.

Number Puzzles

Description

In the Number Puzzles section of the Grade 2 CogAT test, the student's problem-solving ability will be tested as they reason through the choices of numbers that make a given equation true. The questions in this section will show students an equation that is incomplete. They will then be expected to choose a number that completes the mathematical sentence. Completing the mathematical sentence includes finding a number that makes a true statement when the operations in the equation are performed.

Examples of number puzzle questions may require students to perform operations in an equation first and then work backwards to find a missing number. For example, in the equation $2 + ? = 4 \times 1$, the missing part is the number being added to the two on the left side. By computing four times one, the equation can be simplified to $2 + ? = 4$. Then students will be able to deduct that the missing number is 2. Checking the work to ensure the answer is correct, two can replace the question mark which gives the equation $2 + 2 = 4 \times 1$. This equation is a true statement.

Relevance

This section is relevant as students begin to comprehend missing numbers as unknown values and work to find their value. This concept will only grow in higher level math classes. These mathematical sentences will be used to model behavior. These unknown values will be replaced with variables and used to make predictions for many different ideas across different disciplines. The ability of students to recognize and find these missing values will prove helpful for them as they grow as independent thinkers.

Tips for Parents

This section will require students to fill in a missing number in a given equation. The first step is to recognize this type of question. Students should see that they have an equation, and that they are missing a number in that equation. The next step is to solve for that missing number. Depending on the equation, this can be done in many ways. The student should simplify the equation as much as possible. Then, they should determine what missing number would make the equation a true statement.

This section can be tricky because it may require a knowledge of properties, such as associative, commutative, and distributive. The student should be able to recognize these properties and use them to solve for missing numbers. The best way to become more familiar and prepared for these questions is to practice finding missing parts of an equation.

Sample Problem

The following problem is a sample of what students might see in the Number Puzzle section of the test.

$$10 - ? = 2 \times 3$$

A. 3   B. 4   C. 6   D. 8

Explanation of Sample Problem

The sample problem gives the student an equation that has one missing part. The student's job is to determine where the missing part lies and what number will correctly complete the mathematical sentence.

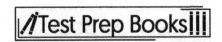

The answer to the sample problem is *B*. Since the problem presents an equation with a missing number, the students should determine which number correctly fills in the blank. The first step is multiplying two times three, which yields six. Then, the student can determine what number can be subtracted from ten to get six. The answer for the missing number is 4. In order to check the answer and make sure that it is correct, the number can be substituted into the equation and the equation can be simplified. Ten minus four yields six on the left side, while two times three yields six on the right side. This math confirms that the problem has been worked out correctly.

Number Analogies

Description
In the Number Analogies section of the Grade 2 CogAT test, the student's problem-solving ability will be tested as they reason through two given sets of numbers and apply the same operation to the third set, where there is a missing number. The questions in this section will give students two sets of numbers that are complete, and they will have to determine what operation leads from the first number to the second number. They will then have to apply this operation to the third set in order to find the missing number.

Number Analogy questions require students to recognize what is happening to the first two sets of numbers before applying that to the third set. Sometimes the operations are simple addition and subtraction. Sometimes the operations require more complex work. It is important for students to become familiar with these types of questions, so that they recognize the operations used in the first two sets.

Relevance
Number analogies can be relevant for students as they recognize that there is a certain output value that corresponds to a certain input value. This will be helpful when they see functions in future math classes. Functions are used to model behavior and make predictions for what may happen to a given input value. Students begin the first steps of understanding functions as they recognize the "rules" that are applied to each of the first two groups of numbers and then follow that same "rule" to get the final answer for the third set of numbers.

Tips for Parents
The Number Analogies questions give students two sets of numbers and then ask them to fill in the third set. It is important for students to recognize what the question is asking of them in order to fill in the correct number.

First, students should notice the two sets of given numbers and use them to determine the operation used in both of them. The operation must be the same for both sets. Then they should apply that operation to the third set. This should yield the missing number. After filling in the missing number, students should see that the pattern is the same now for all three sets of numbers.

Sample Problem
The following problem is a sample of what students might see in the Number Analogies section of the test.

$$(2 \rightarrow 6) \ (5 \rightarrow 9) \ (8 \rightarrow ?)$$

A. 4   B. 12   C. 16   D. 20

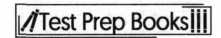

Explanation of Sample Problem

The sample problem gives students three sets of numbers. In the first two sets, both numbers are given and there is a pattern in how the second number was found in relation to the first. Students should figure out the pattern from the first two sets and apply it to the third set.

In this specific example, the pattern is adding four to the first number. Adding four to two gives the number six. Adding four to five gives the number nine. In order to fill in the missing number, four is added to eight to give the answer 12. The answer to the sample problem is *B*, 12.

Nonverbal

Figure Matrices

Description

In the Figure Matrices section of the Grade 2 CogAT test, the student's problem-solving ability will be tested as they reason through the aspects that change in the first two diagrams. They will then decide how the pictures are related and what characteristics of the first picture change from the first to the second. By applying these changes, or patterns, to the third picture, the final diagram can be constructed. The result should be one of the answer choices.

This section is very similar in task to the Quantitative questions that ask to find the next number in the series. Because these questions involve diagrams, there is an extra layer of difficulty for students to reason through. There are many times more than one operation is applied to the given diagrams. It is important for students to practice and recognize how these figure matrices can change.

Relevance

This section requires a great deal of "out of the box" thinking. It is not one-dimensional thinking that allows students to understand figure matrices. They must work to apply many concepts to the given problem. This ability to branch out using different ways of thinking can be very helpful in solving different types of problems and looking for different types of solutions.

Tips for Parents

One important aspect of this section is the spatial recognition of the parts of the diagram. Since this section goes beyond just numbers, students should work with the pictures and diagrams to see how they can be manipulated to find new matrices. Many of the common things that change are the color of the blocks, the orientation of the shapes made within the diagram, and the different ways the orientations change through rotation or reflection.

One of the best ways to prepare for this section is to practice viewing different matrices and the way they are changed. As students work with more and more matrices, they will become familiar with the patterns and ways they can apply them to the given diagrams.

Sample Problem

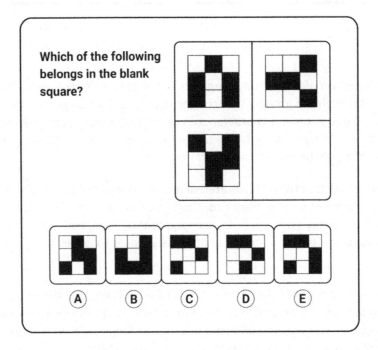

Explanation of Sample Problem

The answer is C. Let's look at the relationship between the first two squares. We see that two things have happened. First, everything is flipped to the right. Second, the coloring has been swapped. So, the black squares have become white, and the white squares have become black. So for the bottom square, we must flip the shape to the right and then change the square colors to their opposites This leaves us with Choice *C*.

Paper Folding

Description

In the Paper Folding section of the Grade 2 CogAT test, the student's analytical thinking will be tested. They will be asked to pick the diagram that shows how a folded, hole-punched piece of paper will look once it is unfolded. Students will have to evaluate where the holes are located currently, where the paper is folded, and how many times it was folded. Then they will have to determine where these holes will end up once the paper is unfolded.

Relevance

The relevance of this section can be seen in how one change to an object may result in multiple changes to the final product. As the paper is folded, it is changed to a different shape. Then the paper is hole-punched in different places. When the paper is unfolded, there are many more holes than were originally punched on the folded paper. Students may apply this knowledge to their lives in how one choice may result in many consequences for not only themselves but for others around them. One choice can be the difference between many good outcomes and many bad outcomes.

Tips for Parents

This concept is commonly seen by children when they make paper snowflakes. They are given a piece of paper and they fold it a given number of times. Then they use scissors to cut the snowflake a few times. When they unfold the paper, it resembles a snowflake because of all the holes and cuts that were made.

A simple way for parents to prepare students for this section is to practice this hands-on activity. Start with a square piece of paper and have the student fold it in half twice. Then, use a hole-punch to put holes in the paper. Starting with a couple of holes will make it easier to see where they end up once unfolded. Once the child has tried this one time, try to have them predict where the holes will end up on the second try, before the paper is unfolded. This type of strategy will get the students thinking about spatial recognition and help them recognize these types of diagrams when presented to them on the test.

Sample Problem

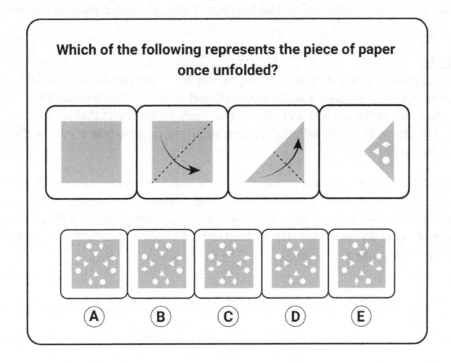

Explanation of Sample Problem

The answer is D. We can immediately rule out Choice *E* because it does not have the original pattern on the right side correct. We know that a circle will be on the right side at the bottom, since the paper folds up to the left, so Choices *B* and *C* should be ruled out. Lastly, we know that the paper folds diagonally across the square, so a mirror image should be from the bottom half right to the top half left. The only mirror image we have in these two places is Choice *D*, which is the correct answer.

Figure Classification

Description

In the Figure Classification section of the Grade 2 CogAT test, the student's ability to recognize patterns

15

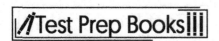

and apply them to given situations will be tested. For each question, students will be presented with figures that are arranged or appear in a pattern. The pattern may be that all given pictures have the same shape, it may be the same colors, or an array of other types of patterns. It will be the student's job to recognize the pattern in the given diagrams and apply that same pattern to choose the next picture.

Relevance

The relevance of this section can be seen in many areas of life. In the real world, it is important to be able to recognize patterns, whether good or bad, and make smart choices based on those patterns. As a parent, seeing the patterns in a child's life may lead to a certain type of action. If a student begins playing video games every day after school and his grades begin to drop around the same time, the parents may reevaluate the time the student spends playing games.

Another example may be a positive pattern. If a child sees that he wants to get better at a certain sport, he may begin to practice every day. If this practicing becomes a pattern, it will most likely result in better participation in the sport and a more positive outlook on the game. The more students can recognize patterns, the better able they will be to either change the bad ones or continue in the good ones.

Tips for Parents

As far as preparing students for this section, it may be helpful to use hands-on materials similar to the paper folding. Parents could prepare a set of materials that have something in common. They could present these materials to the student and ask them to describe an object that would follow the last given material. They could then talk with the student about the pattern that is used and why they chose that material to fit the pattern.

Another way to practice for these types of questions is by drawing out questions with shapes or diagrams and then give the students a few shapes to choose from as the answer. It can be presented to the students as multiple choice. Once the student chooses the correct shape, or diagram, the parent can ask why the other objects do not fit. Sometimes the concept of proving something wrong helps deepen the understanding for a student.

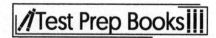

Sample Problem

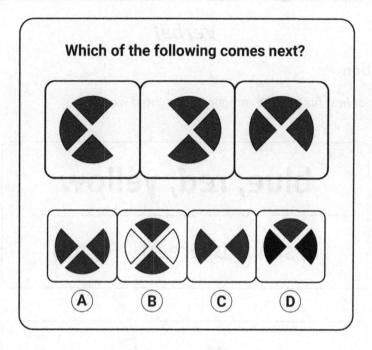

Explanation of Sample Problem

The answer is *A*. We have three pies shaded in the same color. One faces right, one faces left, one faces to the bottom. According to the pattern, we need one more to face toward the top, which is Choice *A*.

Practice Test

Verbal

Verbal Classification

Choose the answer that best fits into the category of the listed words.

1.

blue, red, yellow

a) sun   b) green   c) top

2.

one, five, three

a) cups   b) red   c) seven

3.

squash, broccoli, potato

a) fruit   b) corn   c) vegetable

4.

basketball, baseball, football

a) time   b) sports   c) soccer

5.

tooth brush, toothpaste, floss

a) mouthwash   b) light   c) teeth

6.

shirt, shorts, belt

a) hat   b) sad   c) food

7.

sad, happy, glad

a) confused   b) water   c) car

8.

hamburger, hot dog, steak

a) meat   b) water   c) chicken

9.

sister, brother, mother
_____
a) love   b) family   c) father

10.

lion, tiger, bear
_____
a) animal   b) monkey   c) mammal

11.

pens, markers, pencils
_____
a) board   b) crayons   c) write

12.

Georgia, Florida, Arizona
_____
a) people   b) Texas   c) town

13.

bus, car, train

a) bike   b) travel   c) happy

14.

fish, octopus, whale

a) dog   b) boat   c) shark

15.

grass, flowers, bushes

a) vegetables   b) weeds   c) outside

16.

golf, tennis, soccer

a) sports   b) basketball   c) exercise

17.

cow, chicken, goat

a) shark   b) animals   c) pig

18.

finger, knee, arm

a) shirt   b) leg   c) body part

19.

pentagon, octagon, triangle

a) hexagon   b) shape   c) color

20.

green, red, blue

a) shapes   b) rainbow   c) orange

Verbal Analogies

Select the answer choice that best completes the analogies.

1.

apple: fruit - carrot:

a) vegetable   c) ground
b) orange   d) cucumber

2.

airplane: pilot - train:

a) cab   c) engineer
b) travel   d) tracks

3.

hand: finger - foot:

a) arm   c) shoe
b) toe   d) floor

4.

head: hat - hand:

a) finger   c) glove
b) toe   d) hat

5.

drink: cup - eat:

a) plate   c) order
b) food   d) pay

6.

bat: ball - bow:

a) arrow   c) ball
b) shoot   d) sport

7.

light: dark - wide:

a) short   c) narrow
b) tall   d) big

8.

bird: nest - dog:

a) puppy   c) house
b) kitten   d) coop

9.

lion: pride - wolf:
a) pack   c) pride
b) dog   d) gaggle

10.

school: fish - gaggle:
a) geese   c) birds
b) kittens   d) sun

11.

big: small - hot:
a) warm   c) boiling
b) cold   d) sun

12.

cow: calf - dog:
a) cat   c) bed
b) puppy   d) lion

13.

early: late - happy:

a) good   c) joyful
b) glowing   d) sad

14.

hint: clue - show:

a) reveal   c) open
b) light   d) close

15.

winter: January - summer:

a) calendar   c) July
b) month   d) February

16.

up: down - top:

a) bottom   c) up
b) down   d) place

17.

grass: green - snow:

a) weather   c) white

b) rain   d) color

18.

ear: hear - nose:

a) smell   c) small

b) face   d) head

19.

pizza: cheese - burger:

a) eat   c) ketchup

b) food   d) top

20.

sing: song - read:

a) sit   c) talk

b) book   d) radio

21.

cloud: sky - lava:

a) red   c) hot
b) slow   d) volcano

22.

shop: store - play:

a) run   c) park
b) action   d) exercise

23.

touch: hand - see:

a) eyes   c) glasses
b) hand   d) body part

24.

car: gas - fire:

a) water   c) rain
b) wood   d) tools

Sentence Completion

Choose the word that best completes the sentence.

1.

> **He decided to wear his rainboots because it was _____ outside.**
>
> a) dry   b) hot   c) wet

2.

> **Mom was in a rush out the door because she was _____ for work.**
>
> a) late   b) early   c) sad

3.

> **The pot is hot, but the drink is _____.**
>
> a) cold   b) hot   c) big

4.

> **He decided to hang the shirt up because it was still _____.**
>
> a) angry   b) dry   c) wet

5.

> I could not buy the shirt with my money because it was too _____.
> _____
> a) sad   b) expensive   c) warm

6.

> Martin is _____than Shana because Martin was born before her.
> _____
> a) older   b) younger   c) happier

7.

> Joe brought his bat and ball to_____practice.
> _____
> a) dislike   b) baseball   c) love

8.

> I had a bad haircut so I decided to wear a _____.
> _____
> a) shirt   b) hat   c) clothes

9.

During the soccer game, the players listened to the _____.

a) coach   b) teacher   c) doctor

10.

The test caused Amy to be_____ because she was not prepared.

a) upset   b) happy   c) glad

11.

At the end of the football game, the team with the most points_____.

a) loses   b) wins   c) jersey

12.

The pants were still_____, so she hung them on the line.

a) wet   b) dry   c) pants

13.

> **The boy burned himself when he spilled the coffee because it was_____.**
>
> a) drink   b) hot   c) cold

14.

> **The boy fell off the swing and_____ his arm.**
>
> a) hurt   b) fixed   c) healed

15.

> **The clothes were _____, so Mom decided to wash them.**
>
> a)clean   b) dirty   c) small

16.

> **Strawberries_____on the ground.**
>
> a) grow   b) sunlight   c) water

17.

Joey wanted to_____the TV because his favorite show was coming on.

_____

a) show   b) sit   c) watch

18.

He had to leave work_____to make it to the baseball game.

_____

a) sad   b) late   c) early

19.

Steven wanted to ride in the _____ to the store.

_____

a) chair   b) car   c) bike

20.

The children had to stay inside and play because it was _____ outside.

_____

a) dry   b) raining   c) warm

Quantitative

Number Series

Choose the number that best completes the series.

1.

> ## 3, 6, 12, 24, ___
>
> a) 30   b) 36   c) 48   d) 54

2.

> ## 1, 2.5, 4, 5.5, ___
>
> a) 7   b) 9   c) 7.5   d) 11

3.

> ## 5, 10, 15, ___
>
> a) 20   b) 24   c) 36   d) 54

4.

> ## 20, 10, 5, ___
>
> a) 2   b) 2.5   c) 3   d) 1

5.

8, 15, 22, 29, ___

a) 20   b) 24   c) 36   d) 54

6.

6.5, 9, 11.5, 14, ___

a) 22   b) 17   c) 16.5   d) 15.5

7.

2, 4, 6, ___

a) 8   b) 12   c) 14   d) 10

8.

1, 2, 4, ___

a) 12   b) 10   c) 6   d) 8

9.

16, 12, 8, 4, ____

a) 5   b) 0   c) 2   d) 6

10.

2.5, 6.5, 9.5, ____

a) 20   b) 15   c) 12.5   d) 11.5

11.

1.75, 3, 4.25, 5.5, ____

a) 6.75   b) 8   c) 7.25   d) 9.5

12.

50, 60, 70, 80, ____

a) 20   b) 90   c) 100   d) 85

13.

7.2, 8.2, 9.2, 10.2, ___

a) 14.2   b) 12.2   c) 12   d) 11.2

14.

3.75, 2.5, 1.25, ___

a) 1   b) 0.25   c) 0.5   d) 0

15.

2, 3, 5, 6, ___

a) 4   b) 8   c) 7   d) 9

16.

2, 6, 10, 14, ___

a) 18   b) 20   c) 16   d) 24

17.

4, 5.75, 7.5, 9.25, ____

a) 12.25   b) 12   c) 11.5   d) 11

18.

0.75, 1.5, 3, 6, ____

a) 14   b) 12   c) 9   d) 16

Number Puzzles

Choose the number that completes the puzzle.

1.

4 + (6 + ?) = 3 + (4 + 6)

a) 3   b) 10   c) 13   d) 6

2.

5 + (5 + ?) = 8 + (5 + 5)

a) 10   b) 5   c) 8   d) 23

3.

$$(6 + 2) + 7 = 2 + (? + 6)$$

a) 6   b) 11   c) 15   d) 7

4.

$$8 - ? = 3 + 2$$

a) 2   b) 3   c) 5   d) 6

5.

$$4 + 7 = 6 + ?$$

a) 6   b) 5   c) 7   d) 10

6.

$$8 + 6 - ? = 3 + 10$$

a) 2   b) 1   c) 14   d) 8

7.

$$10 - 3 = 5 + ?$$

a) 1   b) 7   c) 5   d) 2

8.

$$(2 + 3) + 7 = 3 + (2 + ?)$$

a) 7   b) 12   c) 14   d) 6

9.

$$1 + ? = 12 - 7$$

a) 8   b) 6   c) 5   d) 4

10.

$$8 - 6 = 1 + ?$$

a) 3   b) 4   c) 1   d) 2

11.

$$4 + (6 + 6) = (5 + 7) + ?$$

a) 4   b) 12   c) 8   d) 6

12.

$$4 - ? = 9 - 6$$

a) 0   b) 3   c) 1   d) 2

13.

$$4 + 11 = 3 \times ?$$

a) 5   b) 15   c) 10   d) 4

14.

$$4 \times 2 = 6 + ?$$

a) 6   b) 2   c) 8   d) 0

15.

$$? \times 3 = 1 + 5$$

a) 4   b) 1   c) 2   d) 6

16.

$$2 + 7 = 3 \times ?$$

a) 3   b) 1   c) 2   d) 4

Number Analogies

Choose the number that best completes the analogies.

1.

$$(8 \rightarrow 64) \ (5 \rightarrow 40) \ (3 \rightarrow ?)$$

a) 9   b) 16   c) 21   d) 24

2.

$$(12 \rightarrow 24) \ (15 \rightarrow 30) \ (8 \rightarrow ?)$$

a) 24   b) 16   c) 20   d) 42

3.

$$(2 \rightarrow 3) \quad (5 \rightarrow 6) \quad (8 \rightarrow ?)$$
---
a) 7   b) 16   c) 10   d) 9

4.

$$(3 \rightarrow 9) \quad (7 \rightarrow 21) \quad (1 \rightarrow ?)$$
---
a) 3   b) 0   c) 7   d) 15

5.

$$(4 \rightarrow 16) \quad (8 \rightarrow 32) \quad (2 \rightarrow ?)$$
---
a) 10   b) 6   c) 8   d) 4

6.

$$(1 \rightarrow 0) \quad (5 \rightarrow 4) \quad (9 \rightarrow ?)$$
---
a) 8   b) 7   c) 6   d) 10

7.

(10 → 6) (25 → 21) (8 → ?)

a) 12   b) 10   c) 6   d) 4

8.

(8 → 9) (4 → 6) (6 → ?)

a) 12   b) 7   c) 8   d) 9

9.

(10 → 7) (14 → 11) (8 → ?)

a) 11   b) 5   c) 4   d) 2

10.

(2 → 12) (5 → 15) (10 → ?)

a) 25   b) 15   c) 18   d) 20

11.

(15 → 23) (11 → 19) (7 → ?)

a) 13   b) 17   c) 21   d) 15

12.

(2 → 9) (15 → 22) (12 → ?)

a) 18   b) 19   c) 20   d) 14

13.

(23 → 10) (33 → 20) (13 → ?)

a) 0   b) 2   c) 3   d) 5

14.

(20 → 10) (16 → 8) (4 → ?)

a) 1   b) 6   c) 2   d) 4

15.

$$(10 \rightarrow 30) \ (50 \rightarrow 70) \ (20 \rightarrow ?)$$

a) 30   b) 25   c) 35   d) 40

16.

$$(5 \rightarrow 15) \ (6 \rightarrow 18) \ (8 \rightarrow ?)$$

a) 32   b) 12   c) 16   d) 24

17.

$$(15 \rightarrow 11) \ (24 \rightarrow 20) \ (5 \rightarrow ?)$$

a) 5   b) 1   c) 0   d) 2

18.

$$(19 \rightarrow 12) \ (15 \rightarrow 8) \ (8 \rightarrow ?)$$

a) 1   b) 3   c) 5   d) 4

Nonverbal

Figure Matrices

1.

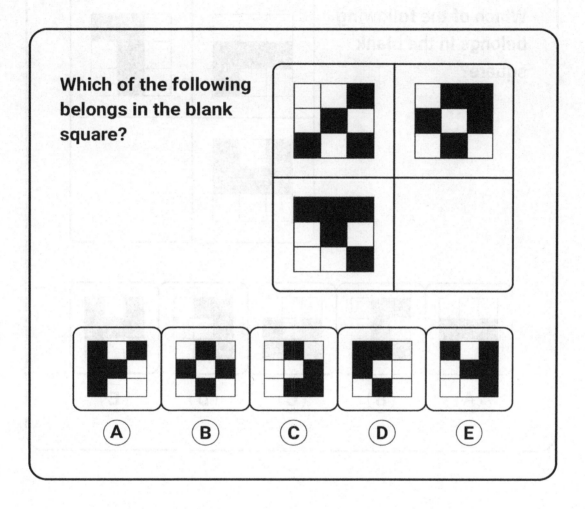

2.

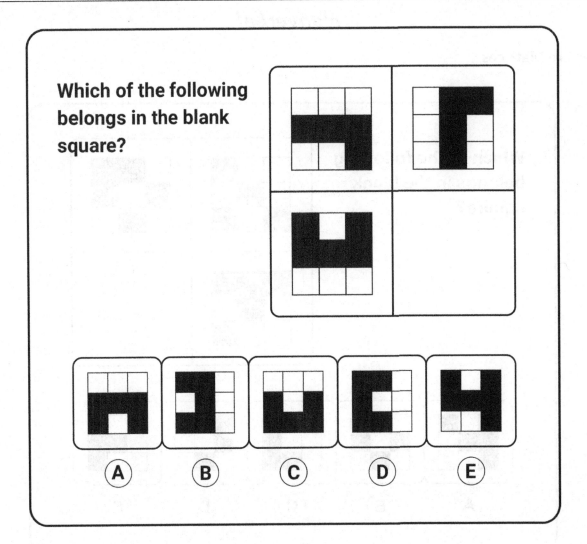

Which of the following belongs in the blank square?

3.

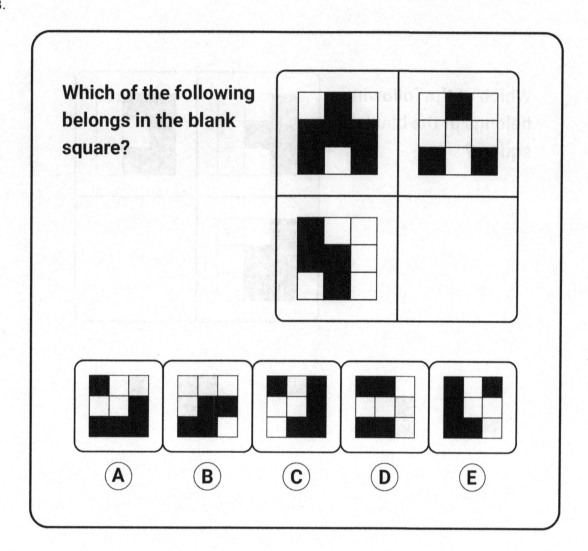

Which of the following belongs in the blank square?

A   B   C   D   E

4.

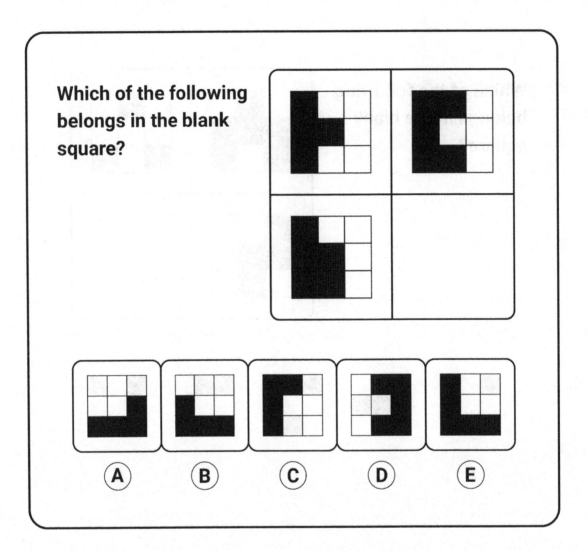

5.

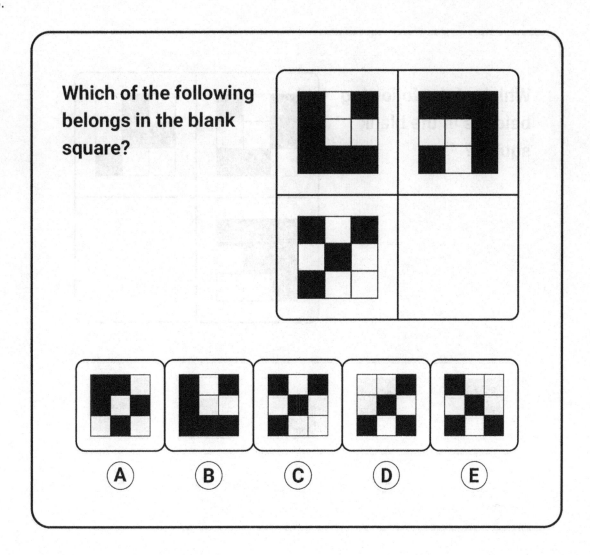

6.

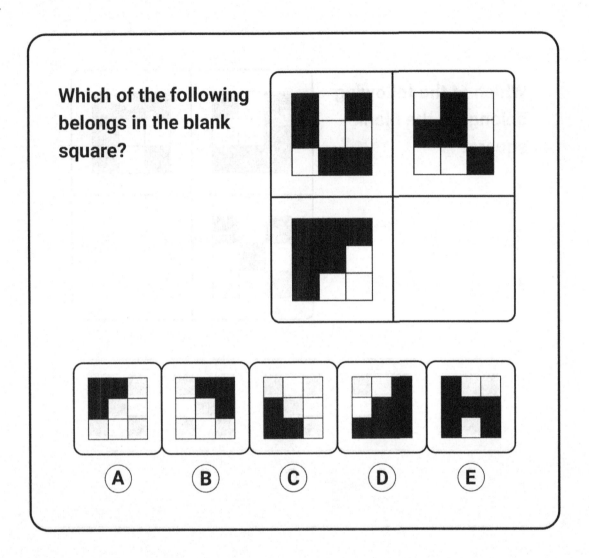

Which of the following belongs in the blank square?

7.

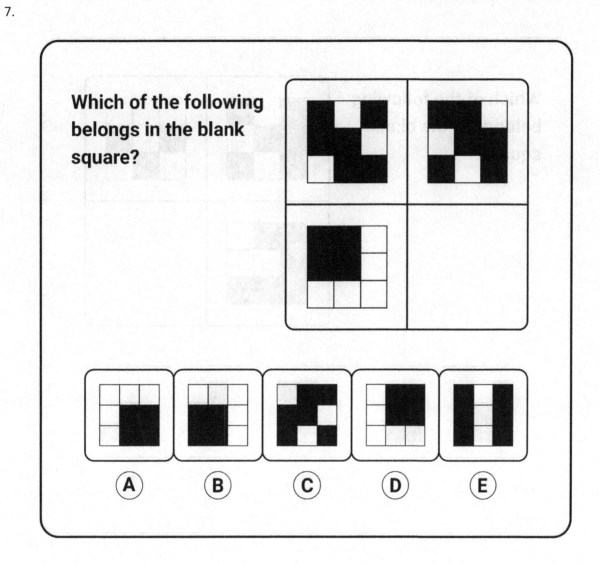

Which of the following belongs in the blank square?

A   B   C   D   E

8.

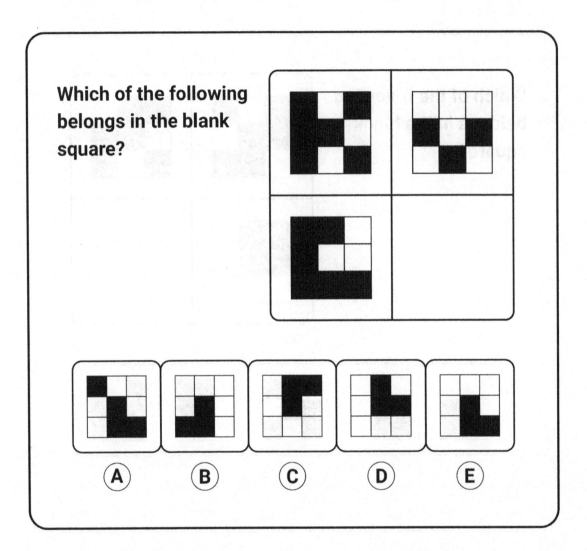

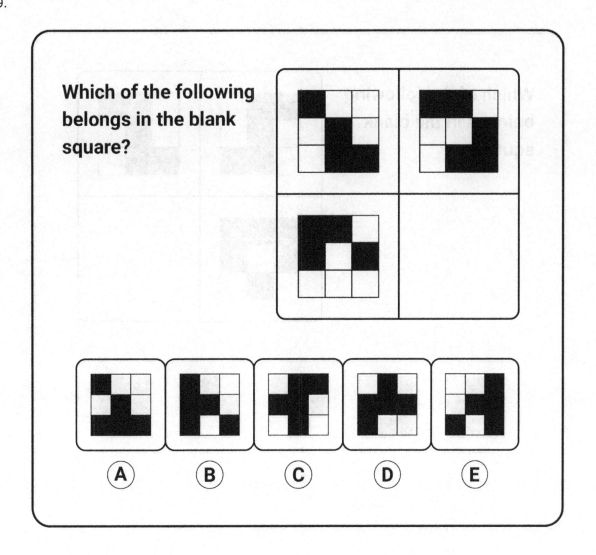
9.

10.

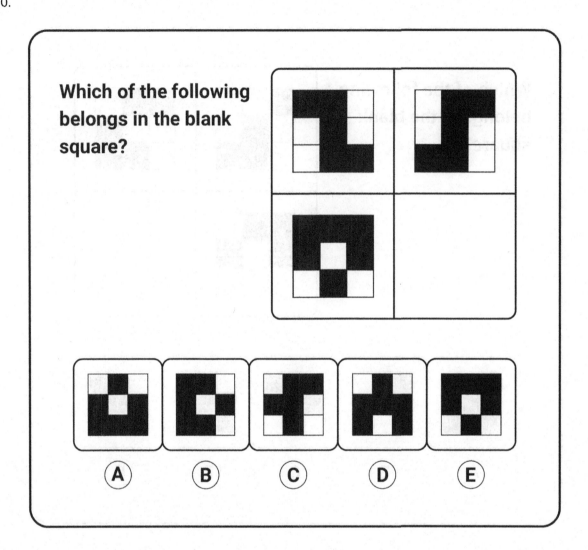

11.

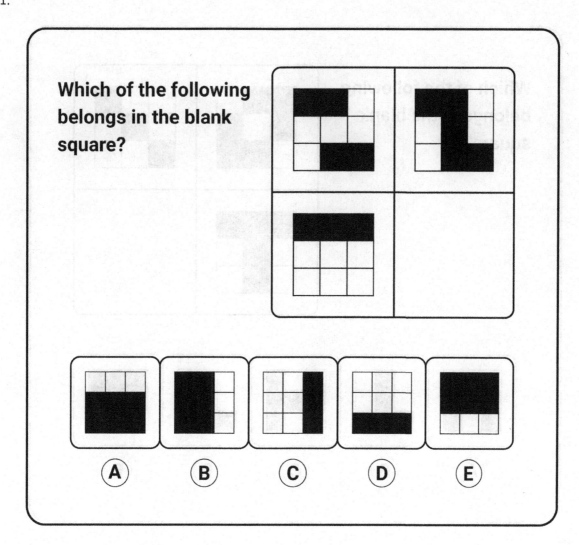

Which of the following belongs in the blank square?

A B C D E

12.

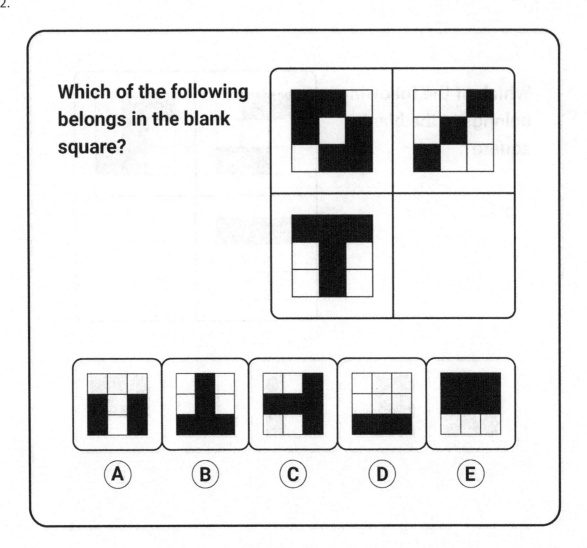

Which of the following belongs in the blank square?

13.

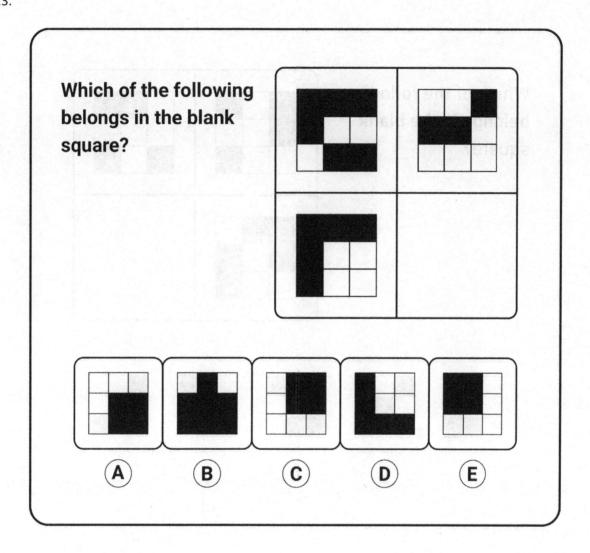

Which of the following belongs in the blank square?

A   B   C   D   E

14.

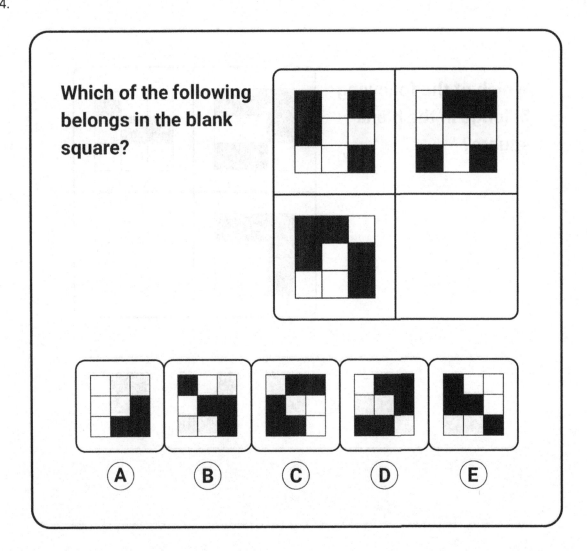

Which of the following belongs in the blank square?

A   B   C   D   E

15.

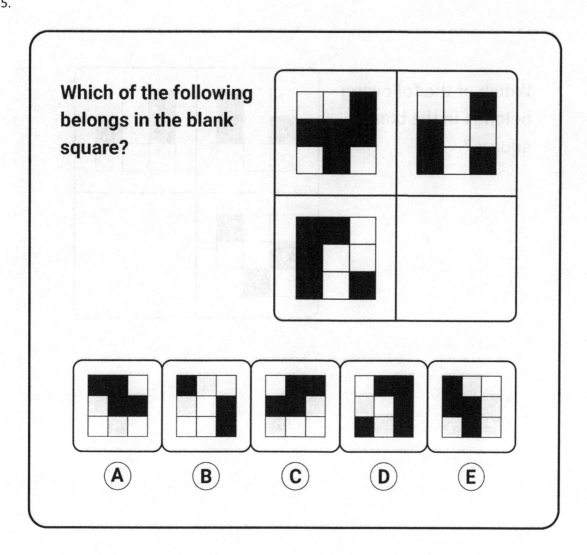

16.

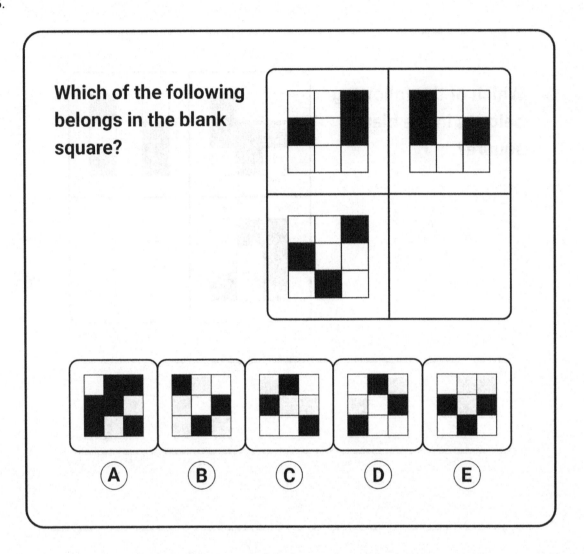

17.

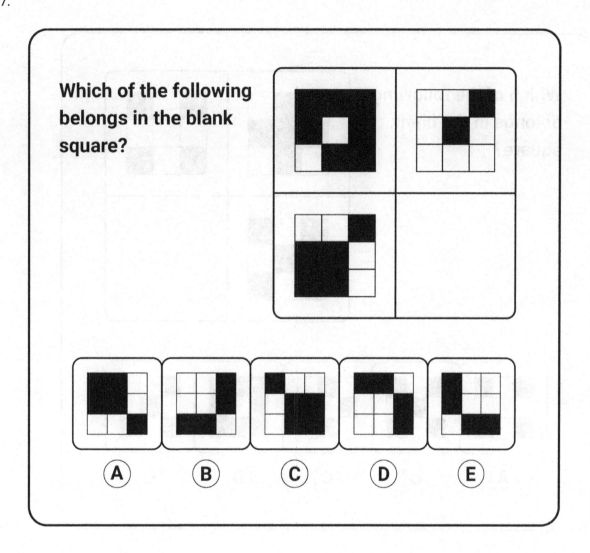

Which of the following belongs in the blank square?

Ⓐ   Ⓑ   Ⓒ   Ⓓ   Ⓔ

18.

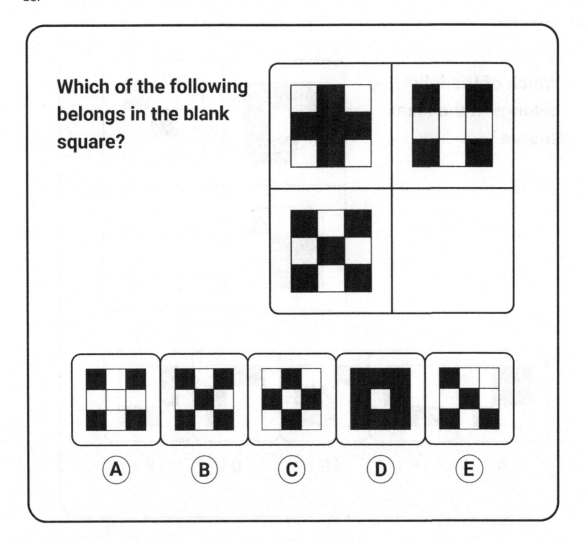

Which of the following belongs in the blank square?

19.

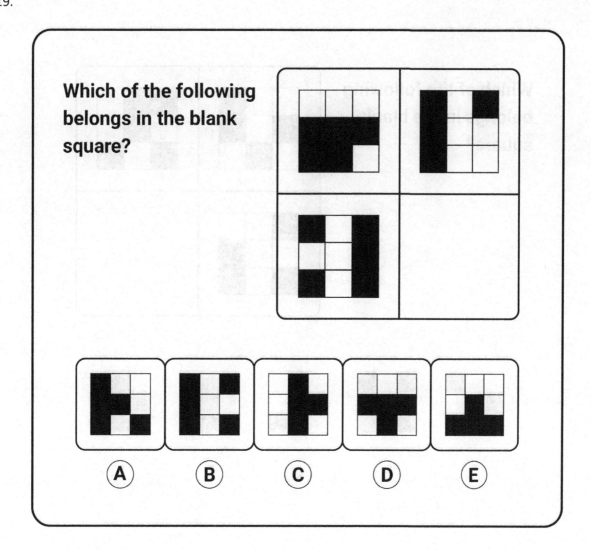

Which of the following belongs in the blank square?

A   B   C   D   E

20.

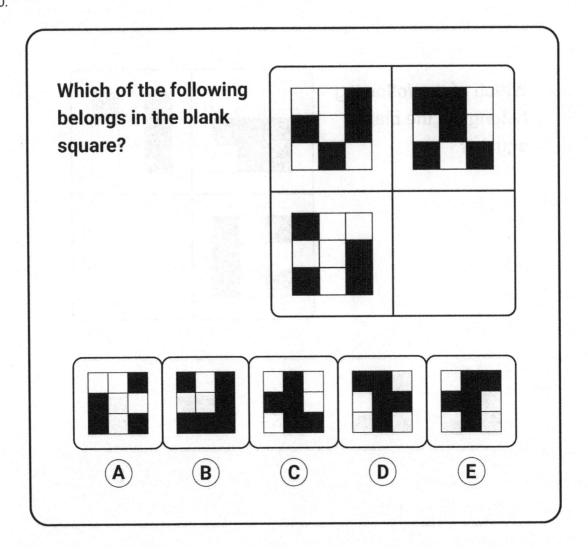

Which of the following belongs in the blank square?

21.

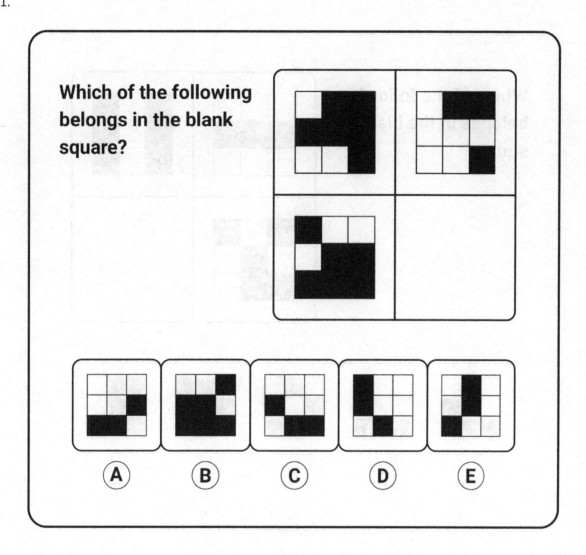

22.

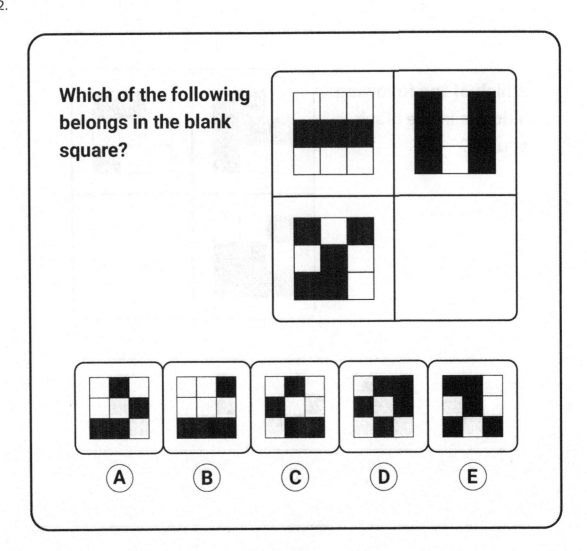

Which of the following belongs in the blank square?

Paper Folding

1.

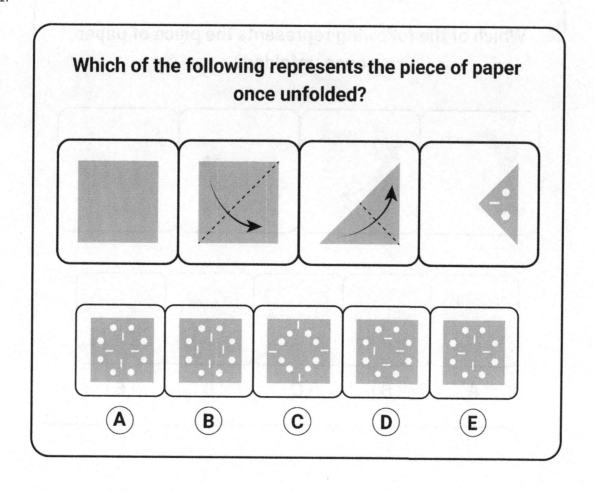

2.

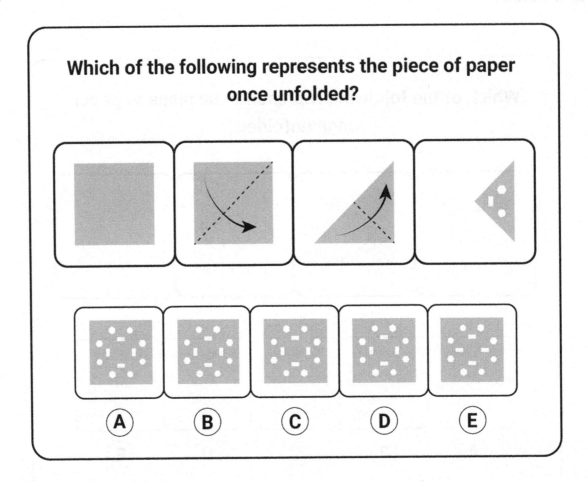

3.

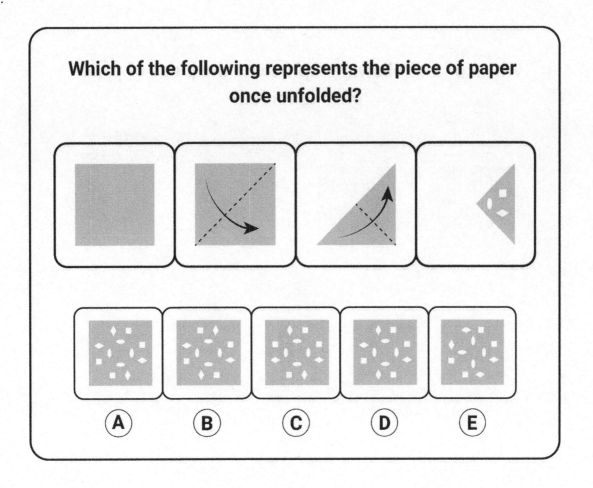

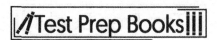
4.

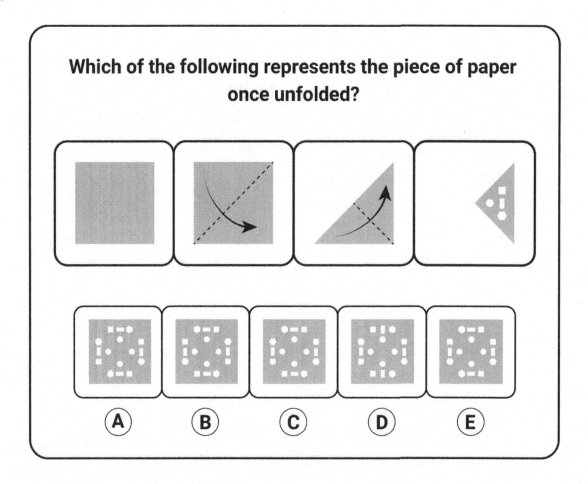

5.

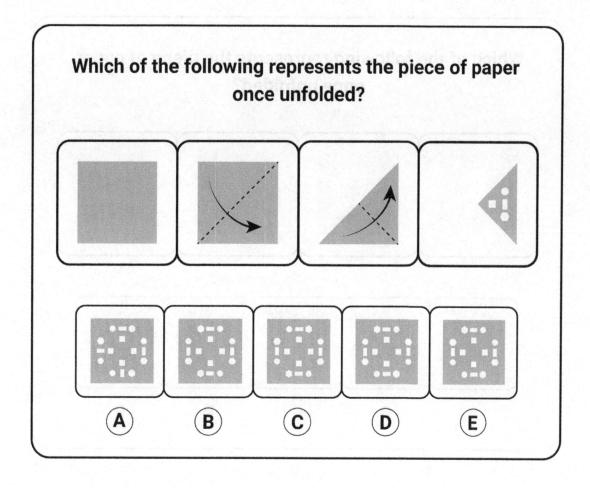

6.

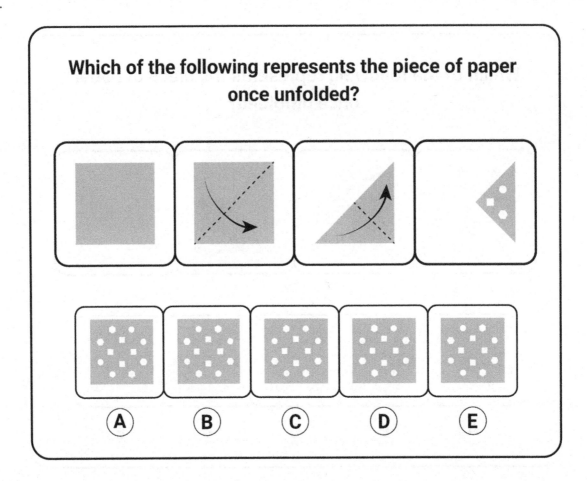

7.

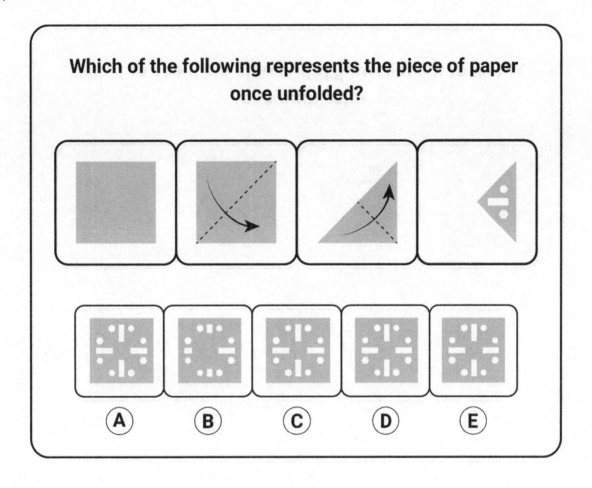

Which of the following represents the piece of paper once unfolded?

8.

Which of the following represents the piece of paper once unfolded?

9.

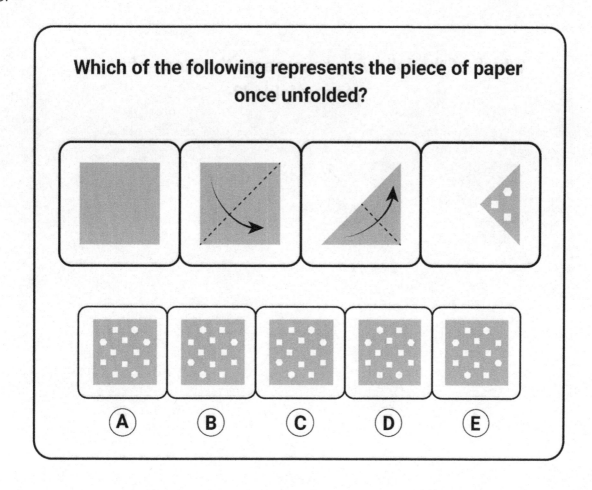

10.

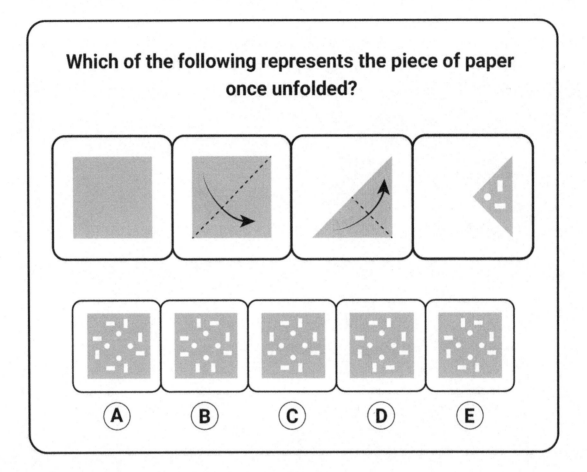

11.

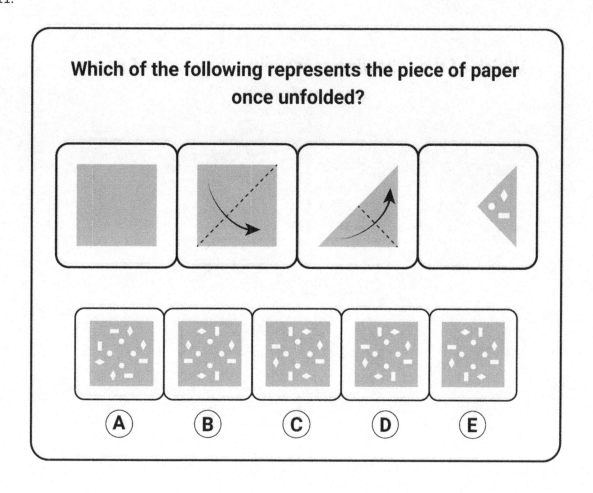

Which of the following represents the piece of paper once unfolded?

A   B   C   D   E

12.

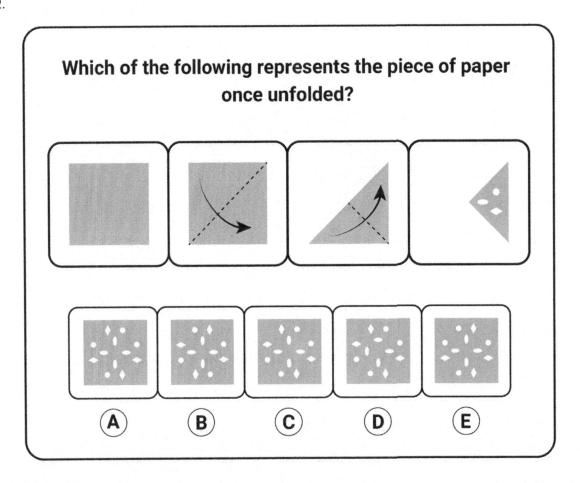

13.

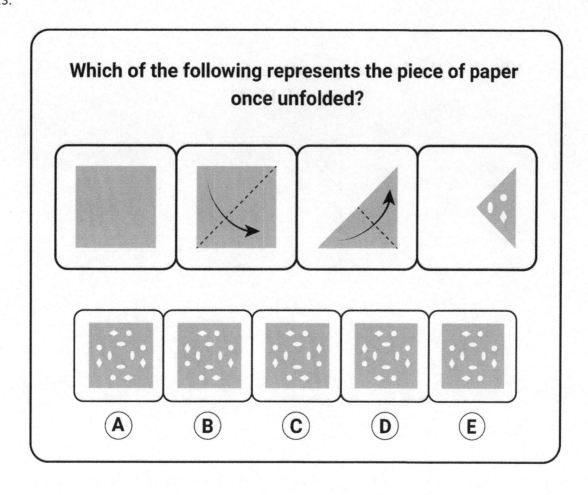

14.

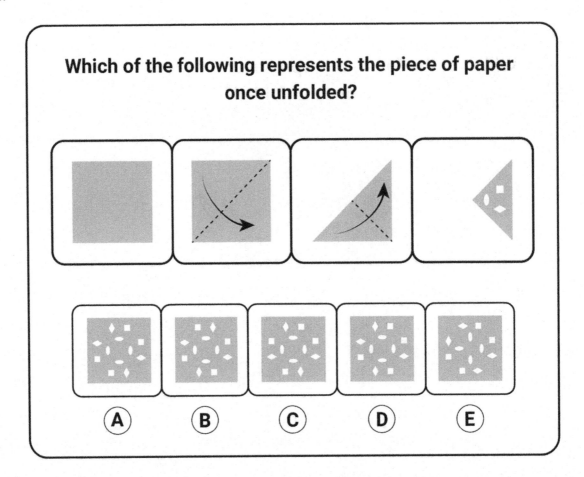

15.

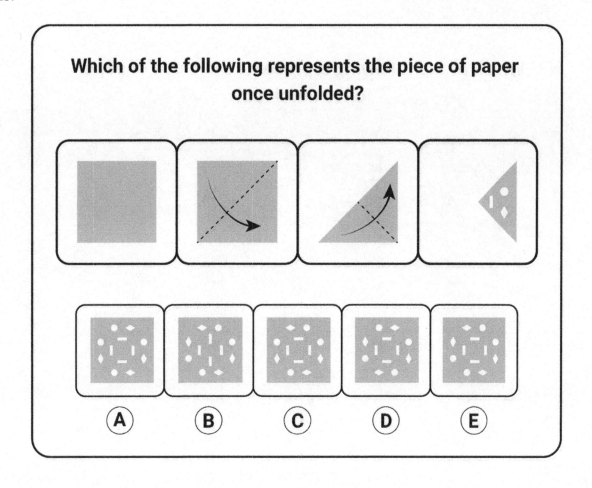

16.

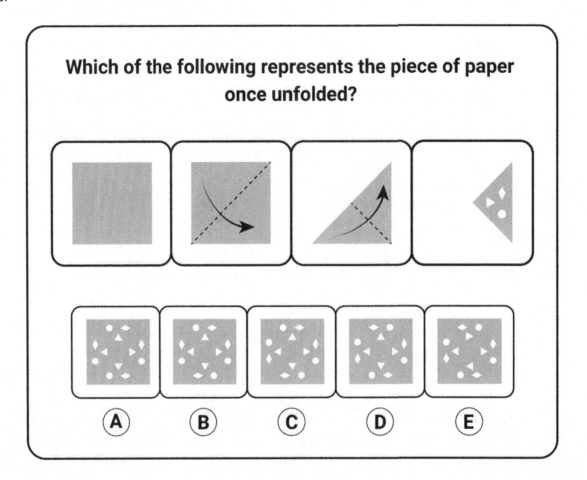

Figure Classification

1.

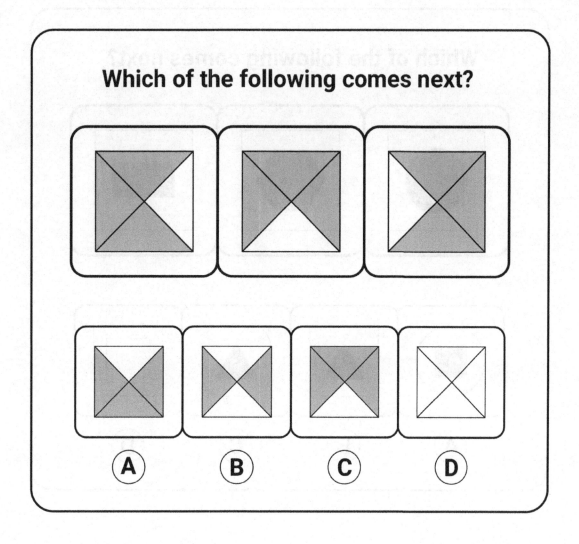

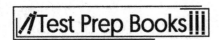

2.

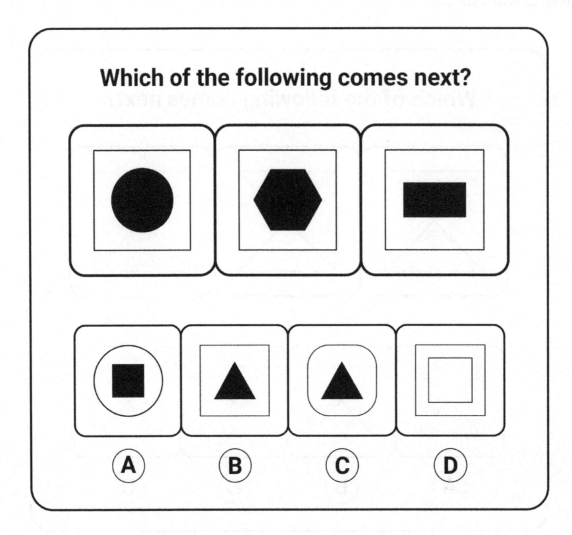

3.

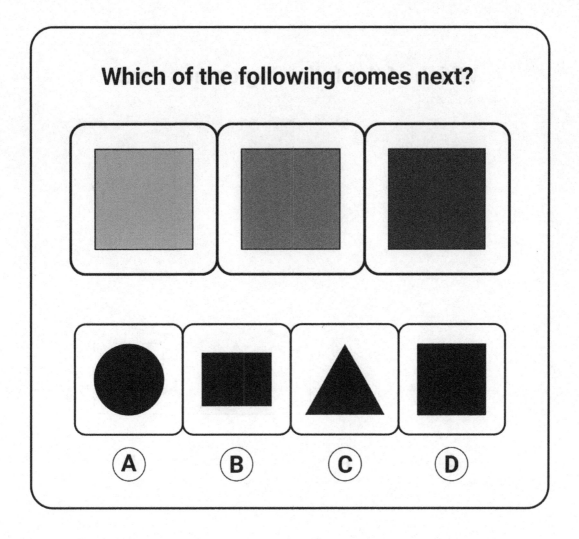

4.

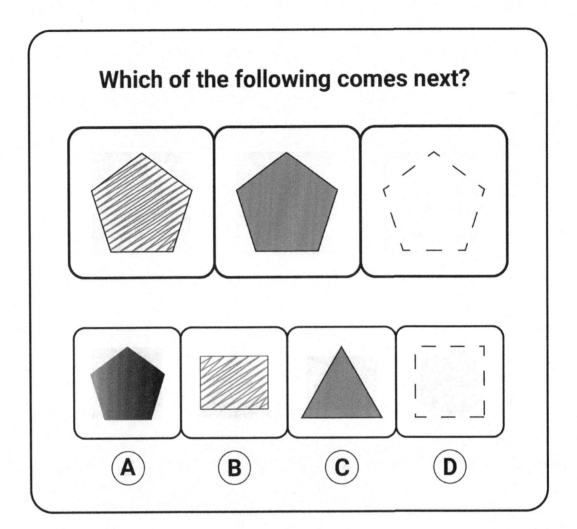

5.

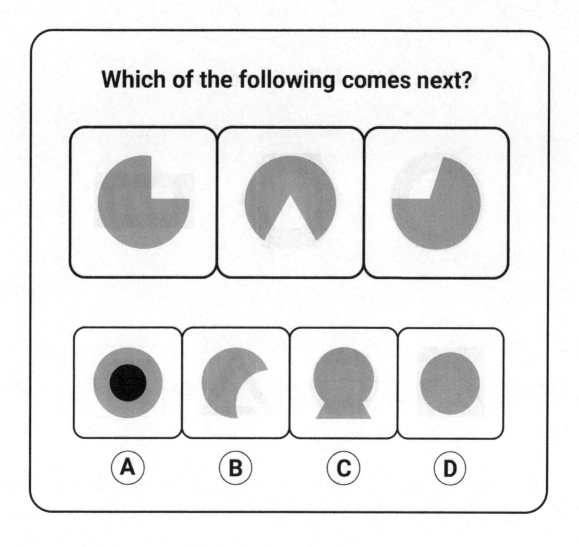

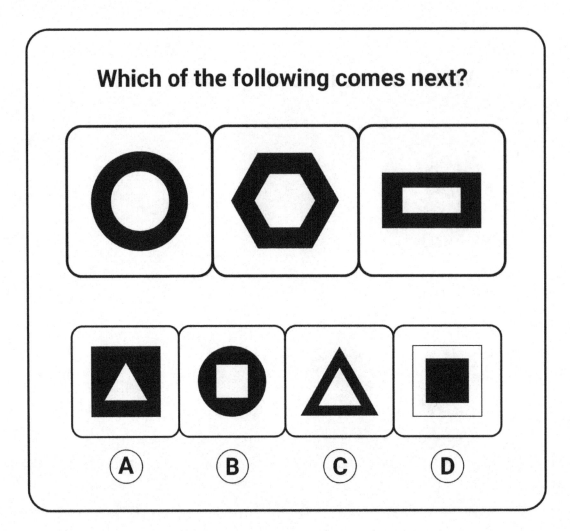

6.

Which of the following comes next?

A   B   C   D

7.

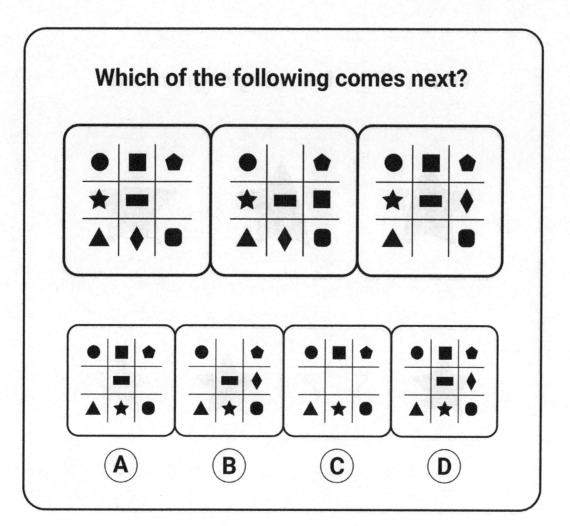

8.

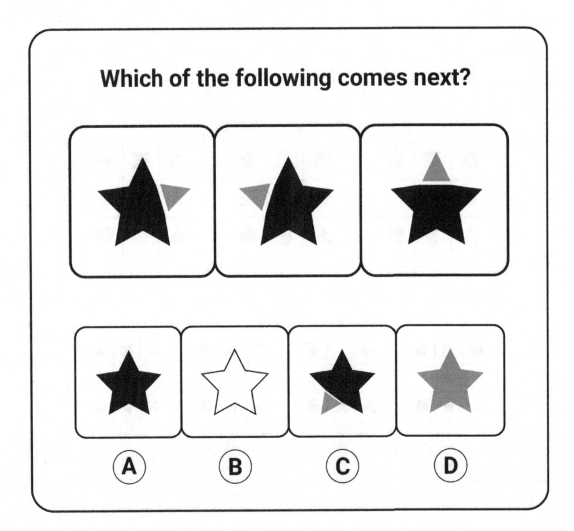

9.

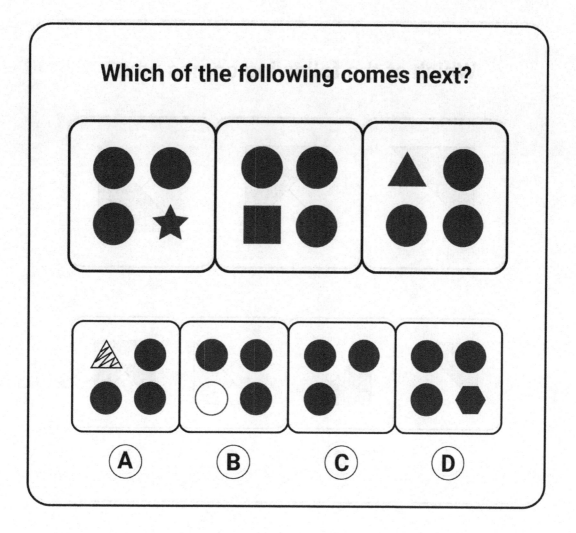

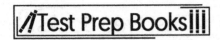
10.

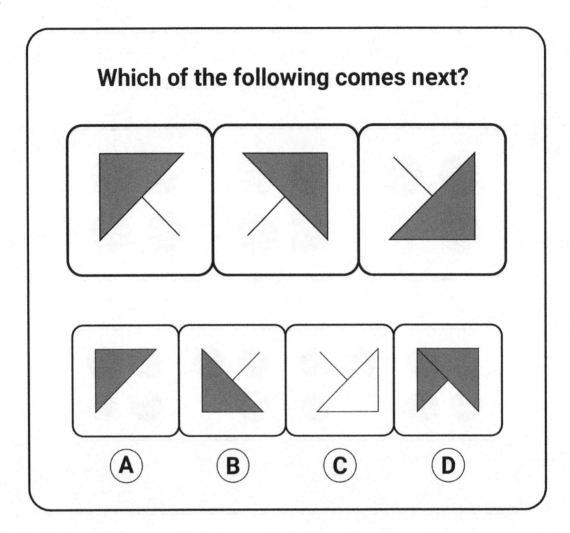

11.

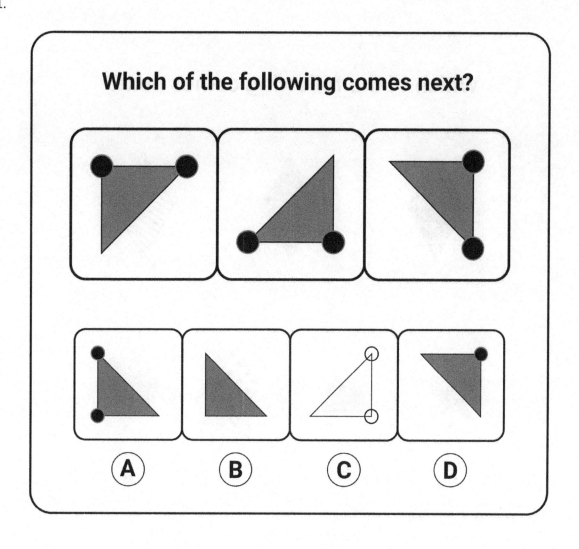

12.

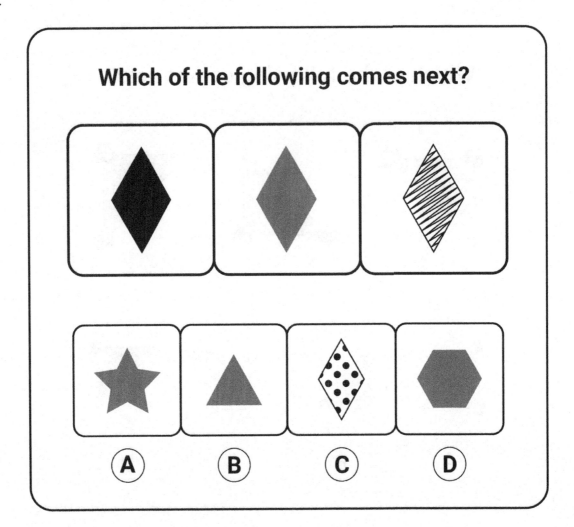

13.

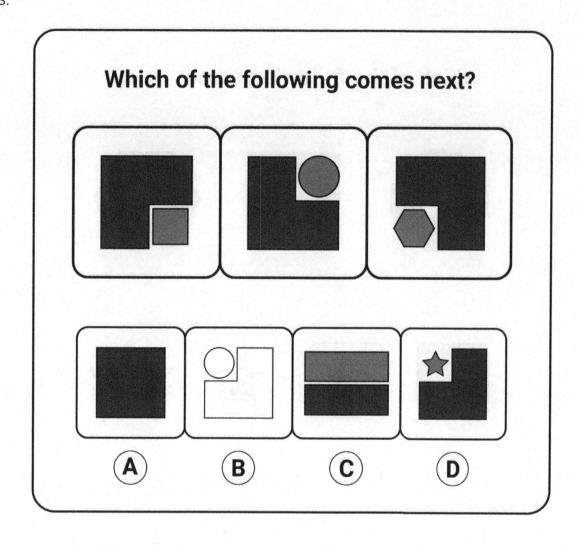

14.

Which of the following comes next?

A B C D

15.

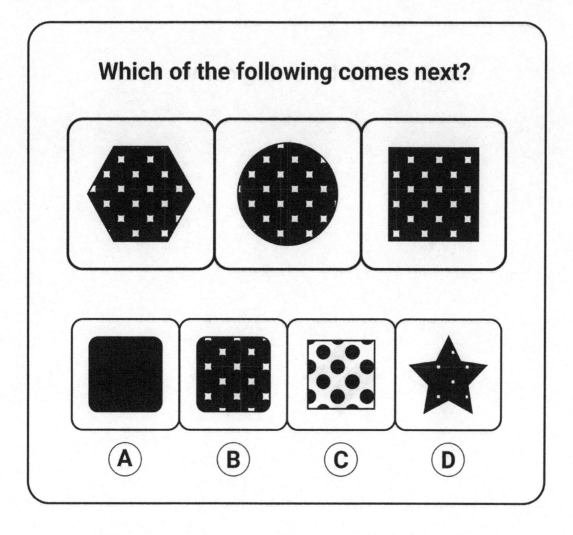

16.

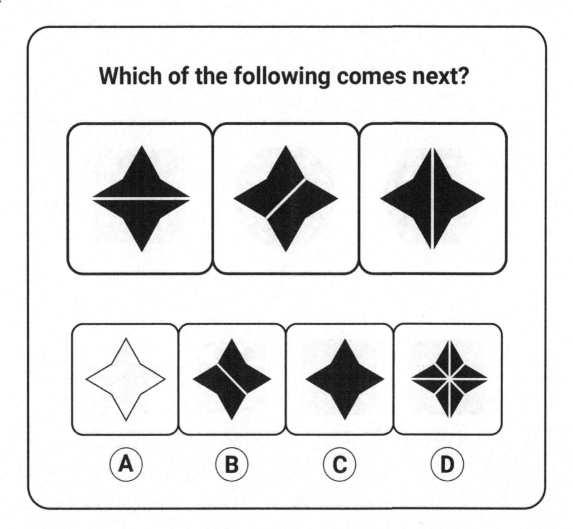

17.

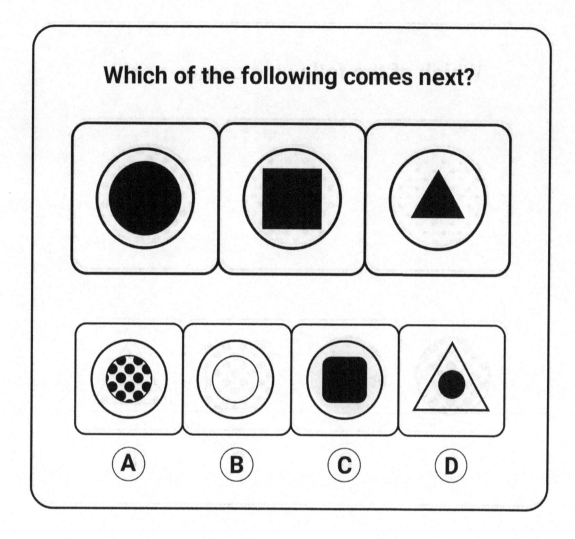

Which of the following comes next?

18.

Which of the following comes next?

A   B   C   D

19.

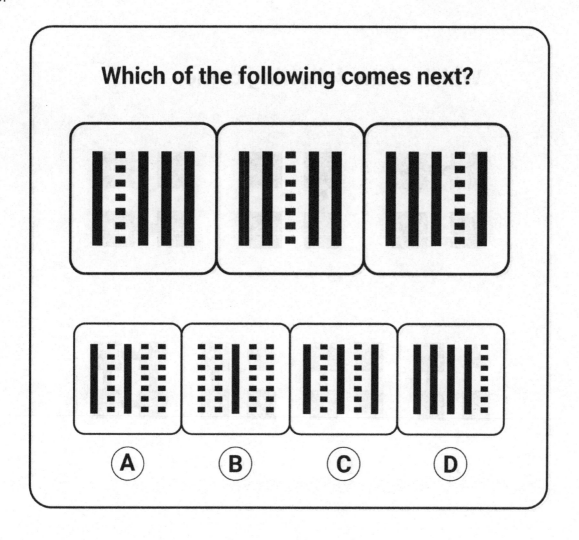

20.

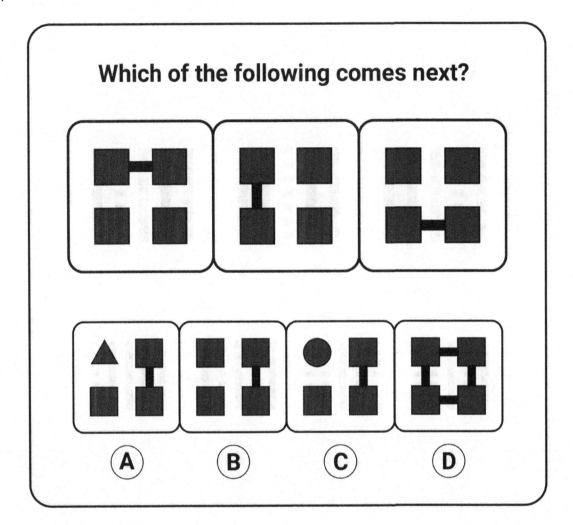

21.

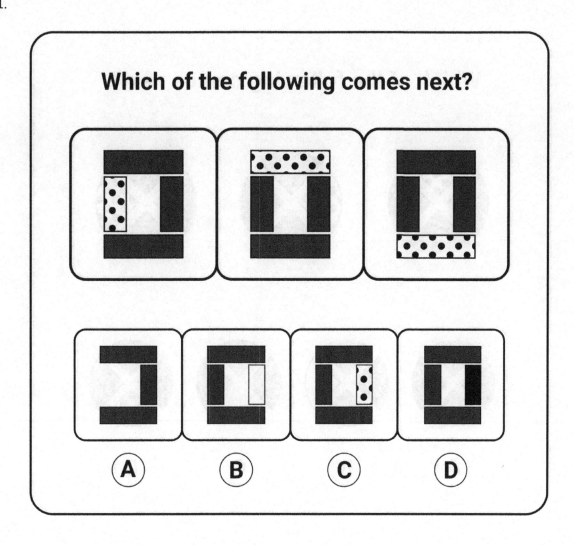

22.

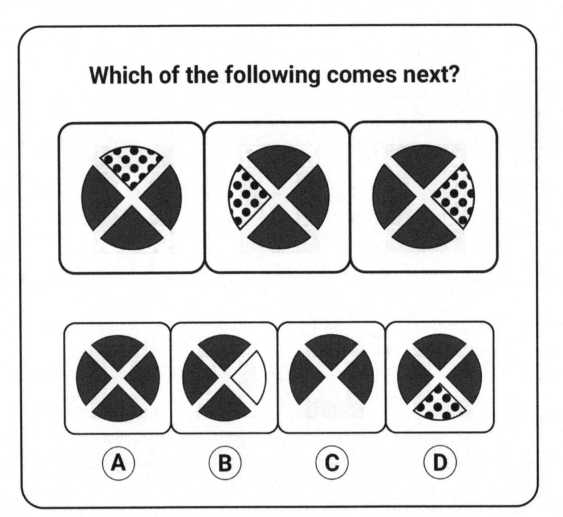

Answer Explanations

Verbal

Verbal Classification

1. B: The words in the given group can be classified as colors. The only color to choose from in the answer choices is green.

2. C: The words in the given group can be classified as numbers. The number seven also qualifies to be in this same group.

3. B: The words in the given group can be classified as vegetables. The vegetable from the choices is corn. While vegetables is an answer choice, it is not the correct answer because it describes the group, but does not classify as a vegetable.

4. C: The words in the given group can be classified as different sports. The answer choice that fits this classification is soccer. While sports is an answer choice, it describes the classification but it does not fit into the group.

5. A: The words in the given group can be classified as tools used to clean your teeth. Mouthwash can be used as part of this group, but teeth cannot because they are not a tool in the process of cleaning teeth.

6. A: The words in the given group can be classified as things that people wear. A hat is an article of clothing, along with shirt, shorts, and belt.

7. A: The words in the given group can be classified as emotions. Confused is a way to describe a person's emotions. A person could also describe their emotions as sad, happy, or glad.

8. C: The words in the given group can be classified as meats that people eat. Chicken is another type of meat that people may choose to eat. While meat is listed as an answer, it is not the correct choice because it describes the classification.

9. C: The words in the given group can be classified as family members. Father is the only listed family member as an answer choice.

10. B: The words in the given group can be classified as animals. The only animal in the answer choices is a monkey.

11. B: The words in the given group can be classified as writing utensils. Crayons classify as writing utensils along with pens, markers, and pencils.

12. B: The words in the given group can be classified as states. Texas is a state in the United States.

13. A: The words in the given group can be classified as means of travel. A bike is also a means of travel, along with the given bus, car, and train.

14. C: The words in the given group can be classified as ocean animals. A shark is an ocean, or sea, animal.

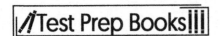

15. B: The words in the given group can be classified as things that grow outside, in the yard. Weeds grow along with grass, bushes, and flowers.

16. B: The words in the given group can be classified as sports. Basketball is the only sport listed in the answer choices.

17. C: The words in the given group can be classified as farm animals. A pig is a farm animal.

18. B: The words in the given group can be classified as body parts. A leg is a part of the body.

19. A: The words in the given group can be classified as shapes, or more specifically polygons. A hexagon is a six-sided polygon.

20. C: The words in the given group can be classified as colors. Orange is the only color in the list of answer choices.

Verbal Analogies

1. A: An apple is classified as a fruit, while a carrot is classified as a vegetable.

2. C: An airplane is driven by a pilot, while a train is driven by an engineer.

3. B: A finger is found on a hand, while a toe is found on a foot.

4. C: A hat is worn on the head, while a glove is worn on the hand.

5. A: A cup is used to drink from, while a plate is used to eat from.

6. A: A bat is used to hit a ball, while a bow is used to shoot an arrow.

7. C: Light is the opposite of dark, while wide is the opposite of narrow.

8. C: A bird lives in a nest, while a dog lives in a house.

9. A: A lion travels in a group called a pride, while a wolf travels in a group called a pack.

10. A: Fish travel in a group called a school, while geese travel in a group called a gaggle.

11. B: Big is the opposite of small, while hot is the opposite of cold.

12. B: A mother cow has a baby called a calf, while a mother dog has a baby called a puppy.

13. D: Arriving early is the opposite of arriving late, while happy is the opposite emotion to sad.

14. A: A hint is another word for giving a clue, while showing someone is the same as revealing it to them.

15. C: January is a month in the season of winter, while July is a month during the season of summer.

16. A: Up is a direction that is opposite of down, while top is a place opposite of the bottom.

17. C: Grass is green, while snow is white.

18. A: The body part that is the ear is used for hearing, while the nose is used for smelling.

19. C: Cheese can be a topping that is put on pizza, while ketchup can be a topping that is put on a burger.

20. B: A song is meant to be sung, while a book is meant to be read.

21. D: Clouds are found in the sky, while lava is found in a volcano.

22. C: A store is where people go to shop, while a park is where people go to play.

23. A: A hand is what is used for the sense of touch, while the eyes are what are used for the sense of seeing.

24. B: A car is fueled by gas, while a fire is fueled by wood.

Sentence Completion

1. C: The boy wore his rain boots because it was wet outside.

2. A: Mom was in a rush because she was late.

3. A: The pot is hot, but the drink is cold. The transition word "but" means the condition of the pot will be the opposite of the drink.

4. C: The shirt was still wet, so it needed to be hung up.

5. B: The shirt could not be bought because it was too expensive, or it cost too much.

6. A: Martin was born before Shana, so he is older than her.

7. B: Baseball practice is a place where Joe would need to bring his bat and ball.

8. B: The bad haircut would be a reason for wearing a hat.

9. A: During a game, the players should listen to their coach for instruction.

10. A: Since Amy was not prepared for the test, she was upset.

11. B: At the end of a football game, the winner is determined by which team has earned the most points.

12. A: Since the pants were still wet, they needed to be hung on the line to dry.

13. B: The boy was burned because the coffee was hot when he spilled it on himself.

14. A: The boy hurt his arm when he fell off the swing. Getting hurt is something that may be a result of falling off the swing.

15. B: One result of getting clothes dirty is that they will need to be washed.

16. A: Strawberries are found growing on the ground in the right season.

17. C: If Joey wanted to see his favorite show, he would need to watch the TV.

18. C: For him to make it to the game, he needed to leave work early to give himself extra time.

19. B: A car is something people ride in when they need to travel to the store.

20. B: The rain outside caused the children to have to stay inside for the day.

Quantitative

Number Series

1. C: The correct answer is *C* because the pattern is multiplying by two. By multiplying 24 by 2, the answer of 48 is found.

2. A: In this series the number 1.5 is added each time. By adding 1.5 to 5.5, the next number is found to be 7.

3. A: The series shows numbers that increase by five each time. Counting by 5 gives the numbers 5, 10, 15, and 20.

4. B: The series in this problem is found by taking half of each of the given numbers. So, the correct answer is 2.5.

5. C: Each number in this series is found by adding 7 to the previous number.

6. C: The numbers in this series are found by adding 2.5 to each consecutive number.

7. A: This group of numbers are even numbers, or numbers that increase by 2 each time.

8. D: These numbers are doubled each time to find the next number. One doubles to two, which doubles to four, which doubles to eight.

9. B: Each time these numbers change, 4 is subtracted from the previous number. 4-0 is 0.

10. D: This series is more complex as the number being added each time decreases by one. Between the first two numbers, the increase is 4, then they increase by 3, and then by 2.

11. A: Each time these numbers are increased by 1.25 to find the given series.

12. B: These numbers are skip-counting by ten, or increasing each time by ten.

13. D: Even though there are decimals in this number, the series is only to increase them by one.

14. D: This series shows numbers that are decreasing by 1.25. By decreasing the last given number by 1.25, the next number is zero.

15. B: The pattern that determines this series is adding one, then adding two, then adding one, and then adding two. For the fourth number, the pattern continues by adding two to get eight.

16. A: Each time these numbers are increased by 4 to get the next number.

17. D: The series of these numbers is found by adding 1.75 to the previous number.

18. B: These numbers are doubling each time, or multiplying the previous number by two.

Number Puzzles

1. A: To make this a true statement, the missing number of three must fill in the blank. This makes both sides of the equation equal to 13.

2. C: The missing number in this equation is 8, because the total on the right side is 18. In order for the left side to add to 18, the missing number must be 8.

3. D: The missing number is 7 because it is the number that makes both sides of the equation equal to 14.

4. B: This equation is different but requires the same level of thinking. The right side has a sum of 5, so the left side must have a difference of five to make this a true math statement.

5. B: In order for this to be a true statement, the missing number must be 5. Both sides yield a sum of eleven.

6. B: The total for the right side of the equation is 13. By adding eight and six on the left side, the sum is 14. The difference between 13 and 14 is one.

7. D: The mathematical statement must have a value of 7, so the missing number to add to 5 is two.

8. A: The missing number is 7 because it is the number that makes the statement true.

9. D: The difference on the right side is 5, so the sum on the left must be 5 also. A value of 4 can be added to one to yield 5.

10. C: By subtracting six from eight, the total of 2 is found. The sum of two can also be found on the right side by adding one and one.

11. A: The total on the left side is 16, so the number missing on the right side is 4.

12. C: The difference on the right side of the equation gives a value of 3. The number one can be subtracted from 4 to get an answer of three also.

13. A: The left side gives a sum of 15. By analyzing the factors of 15, the missing number is found to be 5 because the product of 3 and 5 is fifteen.

14. B: The product of four and two is 8. The sum of six and two is eight. These two operations are equal to one another.

15. C: The sum of the right side is six. By factoring six, the factors of three and two are found, which make a true mathematical statement.

16. A: The sum of the left side is 9. The factors of 9 are three and nine and one. Multiplying three by three yields a value of 9.

Number Analogies

1. D: The number analogies for this problem are each multiplying by eight. By multiplying three by eight, the answer of 24 is found.

2. B: The relationship between these numbers is found to be doubled. Multiplying the given number by two yields a missing number of sixteen.

3. D: These analogies are found by adding one to the given number.

4. A: These analogies make sense by multiples of three. The first number is multiplied by three to get the missing number.

5. C: The number analogy in this problem is multiplying by four.

6. A: The relationship between each set of numbers is a difference of one. By subtracting one from 9, the answer is 8.

7. D: Each number is being subtracted by 4. Taking four away from eight is found to be four.

8. D: The difference in these sets of numbers is increasing by one each time. The third set of numbers is found by adding three.

9. B: Each of these sets of numbers is found by subtracting three each time.

10. D: The analogy found in this set of numbers is adding 10 to the first, given number.

11. D: The addition of eight is the analogy that all these sets of numbers have in common.

12. B: Each of these sets of numbers are found by adding seven each time.

13. A: The difference between the numbers in the first two sets is 13. Using this pattern, the final number is zero after subtracting 13 from 13.

14. C: Each of these sets of numbers is found by taking half of the given number. Multiplying the given number by one-half, the final number of two is found.

15. D: The difference in these numbers is 20, so with each given first number, twenty is added to find the final number.

16. D: Each time the first number is multiplied by 3. The final number of eight is multiplied by three to get a total of 24.

17. B: Each set of numbers is found to have a difference of 4, so the final set ends with the number one.

18. A: Each of these sets is found to have a difference of seven. From the given first number, seven is subtracted to yield a final number in the last set of one.

Nonverbal

Figure Matrices

1. D   2. B   3. C   4. C   5. D   6. C   7. A   8. E   9. B   10. E   11. B

12. A   13. E   14. D   15. A   16. B   17. E   18. C   19. D   20. E   21. A   22. A

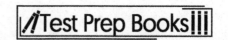

Paper Folding

1. E   2. B   3. D   4. C   5. E   6. A   7. A   8. B   9. C   10. E   11. D   12. C

13. B   14. A   15. E   16. C

Figure Classification

1. A   2. B   3. D   4. A   5. B   6. C   7. D   8. C   9. D   10. B   11. A   12. C

13. D   14. A   15. B   16. B   17. C   18. A   19. D   20. B   21. C   22. D

Dear CogAT Test Taker,

We would like to start by thanking you for purchasing this study guide for your CogAT exam. We hope that we exceeded your expectations.

Our goal in creating this study guide was to cover all of the topics that you will see on the test. We also strove to make our practice questions as similar as possible to what you will encounter on test day. With that being said, if you found something that you feel was not up to your standards, please send us an email and let us know.

We would also like to let you know about other books in our catalog that may interest you.

Grade 3 Math Workbook

This can be found on Amazon: amazon.com/dp/162845749X

NNAT Grade 2

amazon.com/dp/1628458925

We have study guides in a wide variety of fields. If the one you are looking for isn't listed above, then try searching for it on Amazon or send us an email.

Thanks Again and Happy Testing!
Product Development Team
info@studyguideteam.com

FREE Test Taking Tips Video/DVD Offer

To better serve you, we created videos covering test taking tips that we want to give you for FREE. **These videos cover world-class tips that will help you succeed on your test.**

We just ask that you send us feedback about this product. Please let us know what you thought about it—whether good, bad, or indifferent.

To get your **FREE videos**, you can use the QR code below or email freevideos@studyguideteam.com with "Free Videos" in the subject line and the following information in the body of the email:

    a. The title of your product

    b. Your product rating on a scale of 1-5, with 5 being the highest

    c. Your feedback about the product

If you have any questions or concerns, please don't hesitate to contact us at info@studyguideteam.com.

Thank you!

Made in the USA
Las Vegas, NV
30 January 2025